BUSINESS QUIZ

Dr. T. Frank Sunil Justus

B.E. (Chem.), MBA, Ph.D., BOE

Assistant Professor,
Department of Business Administration,
Annamalai University.

Dr. J. Tamilselvi

MBA, Ph.D.

Assistant Professor,
Department of Business Administration,
Annamalai University.

HPH

Himalaya Publishing House

ISO 9001:2015 CERTIFIED

First Edition : 2014
Reprint : 2019
Reprint : 2023

Published by : Mrs. Meena Pandey
for **HIMALAYA PUBLISHING HOUSE PVT. LTD.,**
"Ramdoot", Dr. Bhalerao Marg, Girgaon, Mumbai - 400 004.
Phone: 022-23860170, 23863863; **Fax:** 022-23877178
E-mail: himpub@bharatmail.co.in; **Website:** www.himpub.com

Branch Offices :

New Delhi : "Pooja Apartments", 4-B, Murari Lal Street, Ansari Road, Darya Ganj, New Delhi - 110 002. Phone: 011-23270392, 23278631; Fax: 011-23256286

Nagpur : Kundanlal Chandak Industrial Estate, Ghat Road, Nagpur - 440 018. Phone: 0712-2721215, 2721216

Bengaluru : Plot No. 91-33, 2nd Main Road, Seshadripuram, Behind Nataraja Theatre, Bengaluru - 560 020. Phone: 080-41138821; Mobile: 09379847017, 09379847005

Hyderabad : No. 3-4-184, Lingampally, Besides Raghavendra Swamy Matham, Kachiguda, Hyderabad - 500 027. Phone: 040-27560041, 27550139

Chennai : No. 34/44, Motilal Street, T. Nagar, Chennai - 600 017. Mobile: 09380460419

Pune : "Laksha" Apartment, First Floor, No. 527, Mehunpura, Shaniwarpeth (Near Prabhat Theatre), Pune - 411 030. Phone: 020-24496323, 24496333; Mobile: 09370579333

Cuttack : Plot No. 5F-755/4, Sector-9, CDA Markat Nagar, Cuttack - 753 014, Odisha. Mobile: 09338746007

Kolkata : 3, S.M. Bose Road, Near Gate No. 5, Agarpara Railway Station, North 24 Parganas, West Bengal - 700 109. Mobile: 09674536325

DTP by : **Priyanka Mahadik/Nilima**

Printed at : **Trinity Academy, Mumbai. On behalf of HPH.**

PREFACE

The book has been compiled with great care keeping in mind the competitiveness and the need of students to keep them updated with fast changing presentday business environment. It has been quite fun and pleasure that we authors experienced, while preparing the questions and facts for this book. This book will help students to improve their inquisitiveness and urge for learning which has acted as the driving force behind this endeavour.

Our experience as organisers of management meets in our institution and the expertise as quiz content designers and trainers for management students helped us to undertake this venture to design this book. This effort would provide the guidance and information to face the competitive exams and contests with enthusiasm and confidence. From our experience, book in area such as business quiz is a glaring necessity, as lack of availability of such books often hamper and curtail the enthusiasm of rural students to participate in national level biz quiz contests.

The book has been carefully categorised into multiple heads namely, company, milestones, advertisement, personality, in general and the inclusion of micro areas, like Kids, Maritime, Sports and Automobiles stands distinctive.

This book tries to share successful advertisements, the reason for its success and the personalities behind such advertisements and how they successfully differentiated the products they represented to create an interest into the science of advertising. The book takes a look at how business grew taking different route like mergers and acquisitions along the way sharing the path tread by successful business personalities.

This book provides an insight into different entrepreneurial ventures that captures the spirit of entrepreneurs which in turn should ignite young business minds. Being a book on business quiz, there will be certain areas which can change over a very small period of time perhaps even when the book goes to print, like, the largest and fastest as given in the book. The book just serves to guide students to look into such facets of management.

We sincerely thank the owners of Himalaya Publishing House Pvt. Ltd. for having taken efforts in bringing the book to print and have a special regard for Ms. Sangeetha Rajesh, Editor, Himalaya Publishing House Pvt. Ltd., Chennai. We thank Mr. Yeshwanth Rao, Executive, Himalaya Publishing Pvt. Ltd. for his efforts in getting this work on print.

Authors

Contents

Section – I

1. Company
2. Founder
3. Name
4. Brand
5. Product
6. Personality
7. Advertisement
8. Mergers and Acquisitions
9. Milestones

Questions

1. Which company had to make a recall of its drug Vioxx in 2004, the drug which earned it revenues totalling $ 2.3 billion in 2003?
2. Which company was the sole supplier of the infamous napalm to the US military during the Vietnam War?
3. For which company did former US Vice-president Dick Cheney serve as the chairman and CEO from 1995 to 2000?
4. Which company created the original Mickey Mouse watch for Disney in 1914?
5. Which is the only firm in India to produce the indelible ink used in elections?
6. In 1826 an enterprising Scotsman established a trading company with its headquarters in Madras. After a change of hands this company is presently the ₹ 5,000 crore United Spirits Ltd. What was the name of the company and the person who established it?
7. Which company has moved into the social networking arena with an initiative www.myhumannetwork.com, a site which enables individuals and organizations to associate with causes and initiatives close to their heart?
8. Which company has globally launched Creative Suite 5 master collection?
9. Which public sector enterprise has launched three new tea brands – MIM Organic Darjeeling tea, 'Himalayan Delite' organic green Darjeeling tea and 'Speciality tea'?
10. Which company manufactures Portland Pozzollana Cement (PPC) with the brand name Champion?
11. Its name was chosen by the poet Raghavan Nambiar and it was first published in 1890. It grew from a weekly to a bi-weekly in 1901, a tri-weekly in 1918 and a daily since 1928. What is it?
12. Which Indian company has claimed the pioneering innovation in textile industry, the 'DEO2' a chemical that would arrest the growth

of fungi and bacteria keeping fabric fresh and anti-odour even after day long wearing in humid and warm climates like India?

13. Which company has launched the 'JOOS' brand of lithium mobile phone batteries?
14. Which company was started in 1898 and has its name projects like building the Hoover Dam, The Hong Kong International Airport and the Channel Tunnel, the under sea tunnel linking UK and France?
15. Which is the first original combat aircraft developed by Embraer and which later became a successful military prop trainer with more than 650 units sold around the world?
16. Which company is referred to as Big Blue?
17. What is the in-flight magazine of Finnair called?
18. Which luxury leather goods manufacturing company was started by Dilip Kumar in Puducherry?
19. John Francis Queeny could not continue his education after the age of twelve due to the great Chicago fire of 1871. His first job was as an office boy with the drug firm of Tolman and King. In 1891 he came to St. Louis as an employee of Meyer Brother's drug company. He married shortly and incorporated his company in the name of his wife in 1901. His company used saccharine as its chief product and expanded into the general manufacture of fine chemicals. Identify the company.
20. Which is the first company to flag-off operations after the concession agreement allowing the private sector to ply container trains?
21. S. Susindran a typical home textiles company in Karur district in Tamil Nadu, started exporting to the US from 1997. It soon shifted the pillow filling work from India to the US where it has a 200 strong all American workforce. In 2002 it set-up a base in China and all man-made fibre products are made in China. His company based on a worked out model now identifies the product on behalf of Walmart, Target, JCPenney and Kmart in US, manufactures and ships them to outlets and works with retail floor managers till the product is sold. Identify the company.
22. K. Gopal started a company to manufacture valves for pumps. By 1970 he started manufacturing pumps. Today, it is a household name associated with water lifting pumps in the Indian market. Starting with a handful of irrigation equipments the company caters hugely to industries like agriculture and mining and is one of the first ones in India to come up with 100 per cent stainless steel pumps. Identify the company.
23. Rajiv Mittal was sent to India from London in 1996 by his employer an Austrian headquartered water treatment major, to start the Indian operations. When the parent wanted to sell-off the India business in 2005, Mittal teamed up with three colleagues and with support from

ICICI Ventures bought out the company. In 2007 Mittal again with ICICI Venture bought out the Vienna based parent and built the prestigious Chennai desalination plant. Identify the company.

24. Which was the first Indian company to launch an indigenously developed Hepatitis B vaccine?
25. Manish Sabharwal along with his college friends Ashok Reddy and Mohit Gupta started one of the country's largest HR Services provider which has formed the country's first public–private partnership employment exchange – the Karnataka Employment Centre. Name the HR Services Company.
26. Which is the world's largest diamond manufacturing company?
27. Vikaas Gutgutia started India's first floriculture retail network, with a small seed capital of ₹ 5,000 in 1994 which has grown to nearly 100 outlets, 70 strategic alliances across the country and nearly 160 vendor partners outside the country. His is the first chain in India to offer local and imported flowers through its own web portal. Identify the company.
28. M. Manal saw restless elephants being fed with a root to pacify them which made him to develop the anti-hypertensive drug Serpina. He spent his days riding his bicycle through the forests and learning about herbs from the local healers. This legacy of researching nature has converted Ayurveda's herbal tradition into a complete range of proprietary formulations dedicated to healthy living and longevity. Name the company.
29. Which personal computer company was formed in 1982 by Rod Canion, Jim Harris and Bill Murto, former Texas senior managers?
30. Pandiarajan along with his wife started a HR Services Company with a French term as its name meaning 'my word'. His company is now part of Randstad (Earlier it was part of Vedior since 2004 and Randstad acquired Vedior). The company was officially formed on August 15, 1992. Name the company.
31. Which Ahmedabad based technology company introduced Pi, an e-book reader in March 2010, programmed to support 13 different Indian languages?
32. Which is the oldest textile company in India, established in 1871 and now part of Ashok Piramal Group?
33. Two Scotsmen George Stephen and Alexander started a partnership firm in February 1867, at Kolkata. In 1972, it became a public sector company and is involved in diverse fields like industrial packaging, tourism packages, etc. Identify the company.
34. Which company was the first to mass produce penicillin and is today the world's largest producer of psychiatric medicines?

35. This pharma major, X publishes, 'The X Manuals' a series of medical reference books that includes the 'X manual of Diagnosis and Therapy', the world's best selling medical textbook and the 'X index', a collection of information about chemical compounds. Name this company X.
36. Which pharma company when faced with a shortage of Calcium Citrate that it imported from Italy for the manufacture of Citric acid during World War I learned of a fungus that converts sugar to Citric acid and was able to commercialize production of Citric acid through this route since 1919?
37. Which cosmetic company was started because the then Indian Prime Minister Jawaharlal Nehru was concerned that Indian women were spending precious foreign exchange on beauty products and personally requested JRD Tata to manufacture them in India?
38. Desh Bandu Gupta worked for four years with Khandelwal Laboratories and two years at May & Baker. In 1968 with a capital base of ₹ 5,000 he bought over a defunct company and subcontracted the manufacture of drugs to a number of small suppliers. Its sales revenue is ₹ 37,775.9 crore for FY09. It's putting together a blue print known as 'plan 13' which charts the company's growth plans between now and 2013. Name the company.
39. Ajit Balakrishnan and Arun Nanda after completing a course on Mass Communication and Marketing borrowed ₹ 1 lakh, acquired premises on a haunted building in Worli-Mumbai and opened a shop. Today, it is a leading media agency in India and comprises a creative agency, a media company, an event management company and OOH (Out Of Home) offering. It also runs *India Abroad,* a widely read weekly newspaper for the non-resident Indian community in the USA. Identify the company.
40. This was started as a cooperative society-cum-trust in March 1959 by seven middle-class house wives with a total investment of ₹ 80, its first products being batches of papads rolled by hand on a building terrace in Mumbai's Bhuleshwar locality. Their product has expanded to 19 offerings, including papad, khakra, masala and even detergents and provides employment to over 4,000 women all over India. Identify the company.
41. This company started out as 'The Aircraft Research Laboratory' in 1917 which was reorganized as Nakajima Aircraft Company Ltd. and was the primary manufacturer of aircraft for Japan during World War II. What is the present name of the company?
42. Which is the largest single location cement plant in India?
43. What is the maximum number of characters that can be posted on Twitter?

44. Which airline introduced the 'Everyday Low Fare' programme in order to increase the average load factor which was at 70 per cent in each flight?
45. For what technology upgradation did 'Kelly Moore paints', partner with Autech software and design?
46. Which Dutch brewing company was initiated by Gerard Adriaan in 1864 that now owns brands like Żywiec, Birra Moretti and Cruzcampo?
47. What is the present name of the company that was started in 1895 in South Africa as South African Breweries which later acquired a brewing company in North America from the Altria Group?
48. Which company manufactures the tortoise coils?
49. Which company has launched Ireland's first pyramid shaped tea bag?
50. Who was the logistics partner for Nokia when they offered to replace one million faulty batteries in August 2007, which involved a mammoth transnational effort?
51. Who acquired Biocon's enzyme business with which Kiran Mazumdar Shaw started her entrepreneurial career?
52. Which is the first Indian bank to issue hybrid, which is a financial instrument that has the characteristic of both debt and equity?
53. Which company has partnered with S&T Motors of Korea to assemble and sell S&T's Hyosung branded two-wheelers in the Indian market?
54. What is the name of the urban retail sales and service outlet of Amara Raja Battery?
55. Which Indian company has acquired Malaysia's Sabah Forest Industries (SFI) which operates the largest pulp and paper mill in Malaysia?
56. Which construction company executed the foundation for the Gate way of India?
57. What is the name of the smart basic hotel launched by Roots Corporation Limited?
58. Which company was started post a bicycle tour arranged by John C. Dangler in 1933?
59. What is the name of the sandwich retail chain started by friends Sinclair Beecham and Julian Metcalfe which comes from the French for 'ready to eat'?
60. Which is the oldest air carrier in the world still operating under its original name?
61. Who is the first aircraft manufacturer in the world to manufacture 1,00,000 aircrafts?

62. Which company delivered the 'world's first space consumable pizza' that was eaten by the astronauts living onboard?
63. Who is the largest manufacturer of Stainless Steel and Silver plated cutlery in India?
64. What is the name of the company that was founded as California Perfume Company by David H McConnell, a door-to-door book seller who gave perfumes to entice women and who later found the perfume more popular than his books?
65. John Bissell arrived in India in 1958 on a two-year contract from Ford Foundation to work with the nascent Indian crafts set-up. In 1960 he incorporated his company in the US. Bissell met Terence Conran of Habitat; a leading European alternate retail chain which was a major customer for more than two decades. Due to regulations, he registered it as an Indian company in 1976 and the first retail store was started in Greater Kailash I, Delhi in 1976. Today there are 123 stores and the chain has become synonymous with ethnic trends and is a case study in Harvard Business. Identify the retail chain.
66. Which place in India is associated with the highest value car transaction in India within a short period involving Mercedes Benz?
67. Why is the Qantas Airways so named?
68. Who own's the Eveready brand in countries other than India, Nepal and Bhutan?
69. Which agency was founded by Vanessa Ohri and Jaishri Sivaraman that helps working women making a come back find flexible work options?
70. Raj Saraf founded the mass market focused PC brand Zenith. Name his daughter who launched the luxury brand Vu Technologies.
71. Which clock company was started by Benedict & Burnham manufacturing company, a leading brass producer?
72. What is the name of the global nutrition, weight loss and skin care company founded by Mark Hughes who attributed the product to the weight loss concerns of his mother whose death he attributed to an eating disorder and an unhealthy approach to weight loss?
73. What is the name of the company started by Greg Herro, Mike Herro, Rusty VandenBiesen and Dean VandenBiesen to synthesize memorial diamond from the carbonised remains of humans and other pets?
74. Which company was started by Shivkisan Agarwal in Bikaner, Rajasthan?
75. Which cooperative sells milk, curd and sweets under the name Nandini?

76. With which Chinese company has the Anil Dhirubhai Ambani Group signed a $ 8.29 billion deal to supply power equipment?
77. What is the other name of Central Workshop, Thiruchirapalli, the biggest wagon construction unit in India?
78. Which bank was founded by the family of Devkaran Nanjee under the name Devkaran Nanjee Banking Company Ltd.?
79. Whose IPO did the Indian media hail as 'Black Gold'?
80. Identify this car brand that invented the muscle car model under its flamboyant engineer John Z. Delorean, identifiable by their split grille and red arrowhead emblem in the middle and named for the Michigan city where the company started.
81. Which is at present the only Indian company to own an English premier league football team, Blackburn Rovers?
82. Shriji Arvind Singh Mewar has built a chain of luxury hotels, all palaces and Royal retreats named ____________.
83. Which US headquartered IT Company of Israeli origin has acquired the Indian companies Apar Infotech (which was in outsourced product development space) and Hyderabad-based Innova solutions?
84. Which company acquired Boots Health Care International in 2006 for $ 1.9 billion bringing under its portfolio Clearasil, Nurofen?
85. Which company had acquired Indo Pharmaceutical works in 1995, Recon Health Care in 2000, German Remedies in 2001, Aten in 2001, Banyan Chemicals in 2002, Alpharma France in 2003, Nippon Universal Pharmaceuticals in 2007 and Simayla in 2009?
86. Which is the largest investment bank in the world?
87. Who has launched Ontario, a processor that combines the power of central processing unit and graphic processing unit in one chip?
88. Which company has launched the LeAF range of e-readers and e-diaries?
89. Julian Assange is the founder of a company whose slogan is 'We open Governments'. Identify.
90. Which is the largest wheel manufacturer in the world?
91. What is the present name of the company that was started as Rampur Distillery and has brands such as 8 PM whisky, Contessa rum and Old Admiral brandy?
92. Which company was established in 1984 by Rajesh Kumar Wadhawan as a financial company for providing loans for the purpose of construction of houses?
93. Which company was started by Atul Nishar in 1990 as a provider of process outsourcing and IT services throughout the globe?

94. Gurumukh Das Somani started as a roadside chaat vendor in Ahmedabad's down-market industrial suburb of Naroda. He later opened a roadside eatery in upmarket Western Ahmedabad along with a tag line, 'Delhi's Chandni Chowk now comes to Ahmedabad'. He soon entered into catering and started a centralised kitchen (Food factory) and extended it to a one-stop solution for the wedding market. He has nine bakery outlets and an Italian speciality restaurant named 'Little Italy'. Identify his ₹ 100 crore group for which he is CMD.
95. Which Indian corporate was the first to offer international share offering when it offered global depository receipts listed on New York Stock Exchange?
96. Which is the first Indian company to win the Deming prize for total quality management?
97. Which is India's first retail store to get an ISO certification?
98. Which company unveiled two Facebook focused Android phones called Cloud Touch and Cloud Q?
99. Who has started India's first mall for pre-owned trucks?
100. Hemu Ramaiah while in Chennai's Stella Maris College started working part-time at Taj Hotel's book shop. She rented a space on Nungambakkam High Road and went ahead without a nameboard and frontage for selling books and then incorporated sections for toys, gifts, cards and music. She introduced computerised inventory and billing – a first for any book store. As a backward integration she started Westland books in 1993 as a distribution company. By 2005 the employee base touched 1,300. In 2005 she sold 75 per cent stake to Tata Group and again in 2008 sold the balance stake. Identify the retail chain.
101. Which company has acquired Siva's Soft Drink Pvt. Ltd.'s Fruitnik brand?
102. Which company set-up the first ever telegraph line between India and London in 1870?
103. Which corporate happens to be the largest bankruptcy filing in US history when this Wall Street entity filed for chapter 11 on September 15, 2008?
104. What was the reason that caused BP's shareholders to lose $ 93.4 billion in just 59 days in 2010?
105. Which on line e-learning portal where the teaching approach is based on translating the concept of cricket for an easy understanding of management problems has been started by former Indian cricket skipper Kris Srikanth?

106. Which pharmaceutical company was established by Dr. John Gray and George Frederick Bingham in 1892 that was known for the antiseptic product Betadine solution and Senokot laxatives?
107. Which company is a major bottler of Coca-Cola whose brands include Grolsch, Peroni Nastro and Pilsner Urquell?
108. Why was the name 'Pizza Hut' so chosen?
109. Which company invented the 'T' Shirts, both printed and plain, in 1950 and established a new style in casual wear?
110. This television channel was launched by Usman Fayaz and G. Murthy whose Martin Lottery Agencies Ltd., started the channel to promote transparency in lottery trade. It is a niche channel dedicated to music in Southern India. Identify the channel.
111. Which company has launched lastminuteinventory.com to offer unsold media spaces online?
112. Which company has opened a showroom at the holy shrine of Mato Vaishno Devi that sells chattars, mukuts, chain, gold and silver coins and help devotees to purchase offerings that are as pure as their emotions?
113. Which Indian company acquired the bankrupt US suit maker Hartmarx Corporation?
114. What is the present name of the company that was originally set-up as Central Provinces Prospecting Syndicate in 1896?
115. Which company developed the Flora silk scarf and the Jackie O shoulder bag?
116. Which company's artisans developed a leather weaving technique called intercciato (criss-cross weave) that happens to be the signature of the brand?
117. Who has launched, 'Smart Kitchen' – a company owned showroom selling its entire range of pressure cookers, non-stick cookware, etc.?
118. What is the name of Bharat Petroleum Corporations retail chain which has been an 'Errand Mall' proposition?
119. Which is the world's highest airfield?
120. Which is India's first ever branded public issue?
121. Which Indian hospitality chain's indigenous spa brand is Jiva?
122. What is AFR, which was set-up in Associated Cement Company (ACC) in late 2005 by Holcim?
123. Which company launched the carbon 20 initiative in 2007 which aims to cut carbon footprint form creation to disposal by 20 per cent by 2020?
124. Which is the first airline in the world to introduce the business class?
125. Which is the lone paint company that supplies to nuclear power plants in India with its protective coatings?

126. What is common between Michael Porter, Catherine Hayden, Mark Fuller, Joseph Fuller, Mary Kearney, Michael Bell, Mark Thomas and Thomas Craig?
127. Which was the first Indian knitwear company to go public?
128. Which concrete pumping company set a world record for vertically pumping concrete to a height of 2,345.8 ft. while constructing the Parbati hydro-electric power project in Himachal Pradesh?
129. Which is considered as India's first microfinance institution?
130. Which country's national airline is Koninklijke Luchtvaart Maatschappij?
131. What is the name of the real estate and tourism property development firm that created the two large man-made island Jumeirah Palm and Jebel Ali Palm?
132. Vishal Anand started this e-commerce company that made small town people log on to the net and order branded products by the click of the mouse. It was at one time the only portal to sell two-wheelers and LG Sampoorna colour televisions online. The business model is unique by combining e-commerce with direct selling and has introduced a human interface in the form of a web chain owner for the tech weary. Identify the company.
133. K.R. Naik started his career with IBM and soon started his own assembling and trading in computers and components from its garage like operations. In 1994 he became a partner of Taiwanese Corporation and acquired its present name. He is a leader in the networking interface cards, hubs and modem market and one of the largest manufacturers of motherboards in India. His company is also into structured copper cabling products. Identify the company.
134. What is the present name of the company that began as 'The Imperial Tobacco Company India Ltd.' in 1910?
135. Which company discovered the world's largest oil field (Ghawar) in Saudi Arabia?
136. What is Smaland with reference to IKEA stores?
137. This company bought Halfords a bicycle and car parts business in 1991 and developed the children's world business in early 90s, but sold both of them in 2002 and 1996 respectively. It sold the Lasix' eye surgery services to Optical Express in 2004. It developed Ibuprofen a pain killer and sold it to BASF in 2004. Identify the company.
138. A ticker symbol is a short abbreviation used to uniquely identify publicly traded shares of a particular stock on a particular stock market. What does LVB as a US ticker symbol represent?

139. What was the name of the hard drive and storage solutions manufacturer that was incorporated in 1978 as Shugart Technology?
140. What is the present name of the company that was known as Amalgamated Copper Mining Company?
141. Where in the world is Kit Kat not produced by Nestle?
142. What is common between Hutch, HMV, Andrex, Dulux and Mack trucks?
143. Which is the first Indian company to launch a handheld console?
144. This confectionery manufacturer had acquired a plant in Tanzania making it the first Indian multinational confectionery company. It has also set-up a manufacturing plant in Johannesburg, South Africa. It was earlier the confectionery division of the Bakeman's Group. It sold its Minto brand to ITC in 2001. It's famous for its products like Time Bomb, India's first centre filled sour gum and Loco Poco that was introduced with a tattoo. Identify the company.
145. X is the largest single location cement plant in Northern India and is part of the B.G. Bangur family. Its red oxide cement under the brand name X Ultra Red Oxide Jung Rodhak Cement, it claims has rust retarding properties. Their per tonne energy consumption is one of the lowest in the world and is the first in the country to use 100 per cent petroleum coke (a waste from refineries) for their captive thermal power project. Identify the company.
146. What is the name of the lonely wives club of TCS conceived by Mala Ramadorai which was initially a networking and support group for TCS wives but has now extended to a global network covering TCS-ers in all locations and organizes group activities like trekking trips, yoga and music lessons?
147. Margaret Rudkins, third son was allergic and asthmatic, a condition which made him unable to eat commercially available foods. She decided to bake her own stone ground whole wheat bread which suited her son and was also endorsed by her son's doctor. Soon she started selling the bread through a grocery stall and at speciality shops in New York City. Margaret had no business model but every loaf was made sure that it was as good as can be. The *Readers Digest* published an article called "Bread Deluxe" which gave lot of publicity to the product. In 1961 she sold the company to Campbell soup and became the first woman to serve on the Campbell soup board. Identify the company.
148. Who sold cyanoacrylate to Loctite who distributed it under the brand name 'Loctite Quick Set 404' in the 1960s until it manufactured its own cyanoacrylate which it marketed as 'Super Bonder'?

149. Who were the outfitters for Roald Amundsen, the first man to reach the South Pole?
150. Dom Perignon a brand of vintage champagne, named after a monk who was an important quality pioneer for champagne wine is produced by ________.
151. Which jewellery retail chain introduced Karat meter, the only non-destructive means to check the purity of gold and machine made jewellery?
152. Which company's name was changed to Altria Group Inc. in 2003?
153. What is the present name of the company that had its roots as a regional air-charter company named Tradewinds Charters, formed in 1976?
154. Which company was founded in 1925 by Arthur J Nesbitt and Peter A Thomson?
155. What is COGS and DIO from the point of view of consumer product companies?
156. Which Canadian Oil Company was fined $ 2.92 million in October 2010 for causing the death of 1,603 ducks?
157. What is the present name of the company that was started as GE Capital International Services (GECIS) started to offshore back-office work to India?
158. Who founded the country's first aviation company that was later to become Hindustan Aeronautics Ltd. (HAL)?
159. Why was The Goodyear Tyre and Rubber Company so named?
160. What was the first major product of Kashio (present-day Casio)?
161. The T in the music label T Series (Super Cassettes Industries Limited) stands for.
162. Nintendo when translated from Japanese to English means.
163. If it is IOS for Apple then WoPhone is for.
164. Sheaffer is a brand of pens owned by.
165. *Bombay Times* founded on November 3, 1838 has been renamed as.
166. Who has agreed to buy out Australian Stock Exchange on a move to cut cost and fight competition?
167. Starting from a four-hectare rose farm in Bangalore in 1994, the company has moved to manage 220 hectares of rose farms in Ethiopia, Kenya and India. It is the global leader in cut rose production and is adding 450 more hectares in Ethiopia. What is the name of the company?
168. Who coined the watch brand name Rolex?

169. What is the name of the corporate biography of Sandvik Asia brought out in commemoration of Sandvik Asia's golden jubilee celebration which charts the company's progress in the context of India's economic and political milestones?
170. Which company has introduced, "The Mosquito Killing System", in the Indian market being manufactured by Product Research and Development LLC of the U.S. and developed with the assistance of NASA?
171. What is the present name of Taketsuru's company?
172. Which book store was set-up by Charles, his son William and Clifford, the business was purchased by Leonard Riggio in 1971 and in 1974 became the first book store to advertise on television?
173. The first woman to serve as an air hostess was Ms Ellen Church, a registered American nurse. Which airlines had hired her?
174. Which is the oldest joint stock bank in India and it was incorporated by a group of Europeans and nationalized in 1969 when it was owned by Chartered Bank?
175. What did Hotel Chocolat start in 1998 that helped its style of relying on customers for feedback for its trial versions?
176. Which is India's first hotel to have been granted permission to operate helicopters from its roof top heliport?
177. This group draws its history and name from two music stores established in 1865 by Bernado Xavier and Luis Manoel subsequently located at the over a century old Jer Mahal building in down town Mumbai's Dhobi Talao area. In 1953 the first store, essentially a Christian religious and Sporting goods store was purchased by John A. Gomes while the other was purchased by him six years later. The Gomes family still holds 70 per cent in this music venture having 14 stores, franchises and showrooms in North and South India. Identify the music store chain.
178. The upcoming film *'The Social Network'* is about which internet phenomenon?
179. Which not-for-profit venture, has set-up an initiative called the India-Japan Initiative (IJI) to help Indian and Japanese companies do business with each other with two broad areas of focus, business and culture – the former includes manufacturing and IT and the latter ranges from teaching Japanese women to wear a sari to sake appreciation?
180. Uniball is a brand of pen and pencils made by _________.
181. Daily Bread founded in 2003 by Arjun Sekri is a wholly-owned subsidiary of _________.

182. Which company was established at la Ferte'-Milon in France and is a leader in writing instruments, presently headquartered in Valence?
183. Which diagnostic equipment company launched project DISHA a telemedicine initiative in association with ISRO and Apollo in July 2005?
184. Which is the world's largest family run spirit company?
185. Which is the largest pencil manufacturing company in India?
186. What was the name of the company Exide when it was started in 1888?
187. D. Sudhakhar Reddy, member of the promoter family of Oriental Hotels Ltd. has started a bakery chain, named ___________.
188. For which company did Frank Peters create the In-Er Seal Package which is a system of inter-folded wax paper and cardboard to "seal in the freshness" of the product?
189. Which company introduced King Cola?
190. Which company was founded based on Sven Wingqvist's 1907 Swedish patent for a multi-row self-aligning radial ball bearing?
191. Which company traces its history to the formation of Norwich Union by Thomas Bignold in 1797 and the commercial union in 1861?
192. Which company is credited with designing the first men's underwear brief in 1934, introducing the first men's underwear print advertisement, organizing the first underwear fashion show and designing special long underwear for NASA astronauts?
193. What is business model of the Miami based website www.bagborrowsteal.com?
194. In May 1860 the French Ministry of finance permitted the Comptoir d'Escompte de Paris (CNEP), a joint stock bank which was set-up in 1848, by a special decree to create branches overseas, for the first time in Shanghai, Calcutta and Bombay. In 1913, CNEP was merged with a French bank Banque Nationale pour le Commerce et I'Industrie to form the Banque Nationale de Paris which in 1999 bid for another bank to form the present outfit which has completed 150 years of its existence in India with eight branches the first having been started in the present-day Kolkata _________.
195. Which company donated 500 2 GB flash drives to underprivileged children in India through their partner Bharti Foundation as part of their Satya Bharti School Programme?
196. What is the present name of the company registered in 1984 by a Houston born man as 'PCs Limited' to sell personal computers directly to consumers, saving the costs of an indirect retail channel?

197. Which among the present twenty-two private life insurance companies in India is as on date the only company that does not have a foreign partner and operates as a standalone company?
198. Which scheme was launched by ITC to inculcate the habit of segregating waste and increasing the level of recycling garbage?
199. The used and pre-owned car business of which Indian company is named "True Value"?
200. Which company launched the world's first Hepatitis A vaccine?
201. What does the McDonalds motto of 'QSC' stand for?
202. For which technology was there a battle between Bajaj and TVS when TVS planned to launch the Flame motorcycle?
203. What is the present name of the company that was started as 'Ideal' in Berlin in 1923?
204. Which mercantile institution was set-up by Sardar Dayal Singh Majithia in Lahore, with an emblem of three mountain peaks?
205. Which is the first ever company in India to be taken over by its workers union?
206. Which company created the first mass produced pocket watch and the first pocket watch with two time zones?
207. What is the name of the restaurant chain that was started as Bell's Drive-in by Marine Glen Bell?
208. This Japanese company entered India as a joint venture with Kalyani Group but could not use its name as a Bangalore based Indian company was using the same and hence retailed its product under the name Optonica. Later it freed its brand name through an out of court settlement with that company. Identify this Japanese concern.
209. Which is India's only higher education NBFC and which was started by Anil and Ajay Bohra?
210. Which group owns the speciality retail chain 'Mom & Me' that caters to the need of pregnant women, young mothers, infants and children?
211. What is the name of the online retail company founded by Gap Inc. in 2006?
212. Which company first exploited the opportunity to reach Indian homes with water purifier at affordable rates?
213. Which company developed the solar powered Gramateller Duo ATMs?
214. Which group has introduced the super-luxury bus concept "Konferenz on Wheels"?
215. Which Swiss based company introduced limited edition of divinity pens embodying Ganesha, Shiva and Buddha?

216. Which company's initiative is Corporate Service Corps (CSC) that combines Leadership Development and Corporate Social Responsibility?
217. Connect Hino Motors, Scion, Daihatsu, Highlander and Tundra to a giant umbrella company.
218. Which mobile operator in India first offered Third Generation services?
219. This Italian company was founded by two brothers in 1934 and engaged in design and manufacture of menswear and accessories and is today run by the second and third generation of the family. The present marketing director is credited for taking the brand to Canada and Mexico and is today the only player in the Italian province around Milan. It entered India and has partnered with Genesis Luxury Pvt. Ltd. Name the company and the person.
220. Which company's venture is Megamart?
221. This company is the world's second largest professional services firm. Its consultancy business was absorbed into IBM Global Business Services in the year 2002. In September 2010, the name was shortened as PwC as a result of brand repositioning with an introduction of new logo. Name the company.
222. The Korean Lak-Hui chemicals established into plastic industry with Goldstar Co. Later they merged to form this company. Name it.
223. Which airline was acquired by Kalanidhi Maran, The Sun Group and has become a part of Kal Airways?
224. Which company owns the chain of skin care facilities with the brand name of "Kaya Skin Clinic"?
225. This company was started in 1929 when Radio Corporation of America started a UK branch called RCA Services to support the cinema industry. It runs, trains, operates hospitals, schools and prisons and manages air traffic control systems and missile defence systems on behalf of governments. It is said to employ more scientists in UK than anyone else. In 2008 it acquired 60 per cent stake in Infovision and increased its presence in India with the acquisition of Intelenet. Identify the company.
226. What is the name of the shell company set-up by ex-McKinsey head Rajat Gupta?

Answers

1. Merck {the drug was known to double the risk of sudden cardiac attacks leading to deaths than those who took Celebrex (Vioxx's main rival)}
2. Dow Chemical

3. Halliburton
4. Timex
5. Mysore Paints and Varnish Ltd.
6. McDowell & Co. and Angus McDowell
7. CISCO
8. Adobe
9. Andrew Yule Company
10. Prism Cement
11. Malayala Manorama
12. Vimal
13. Okaya Power Group (OPG)
14. Bechtel
15. Tucano
16. IBM
17. Blue Wings
18. Hidesign (He started his venture as a hobby, a one man artisan shop in 1978 and still teaches students at Auroville on Intenational affairs).
19. Monsanto
20. Gateway Distriparks (the wagon used were still of Concor (Container Corporation of India))
21. Sabare International
22. CRI Pumps (Coimbatore's Rajendran Industries)
23. VA Tech Wabag
24. Hyderabad based Shantha Biotechnics in 1997
25. Teamlease
26. The Antwerp headquartered $ 1.8 billion Rosyblue Group
27. Ferns 'N' Petals
28. Himalaya Drug Company
29. Compaq Computer Corporation
30. Ma Foi
31. Infibeam
32. Morarjee Textiles (formerly the Morarjee Goculdas Spinning and Weaving Co.)
33. Balmer Lawrie (George Stephen Balmer and Alexander Lawrie)
34. Eli Lilly and Company
35. Merck
36. Pfizer

37. Lakme
38. Lupin
39. Rediffusion
40. Shri Mahila Griha Udyog Ltd. makers of Lijjat Papad
41. Fiji Heavy Industries
42. Vasavadatta cement section
43. 140
44. Malaysian Airlines
45. Click & Paint V3, that helps customers to visualize the way their house will look post-painting
46. Heineken
47. SABMiller
48. Bombay Chemicals
49. Lyons Tea
50. DHL
51. The world's largest enzyme company, Novozyme
52. UCO Bank
53. Garware Bestretch makers of latex and rubber products
54. Pitstop
55. BILT
56. Gammon India
57. Ginger
58. SITA (Students International Travel Association)
59. Pret A Manger
60. KLM
61. Cessna
62. Pizza Hut
63. Kishco, its new cookware plant at Nashik has an in-house facility for manufacturing hard anodized ware, non-stick ware, pressure cookers, etc.
64. Avon
65. Fab India
66. Aurangabad where Mercedes Benz sold 150 cars to a group of customers valued at close to ₹ 150 crore
67. Queensland and Northern Territory Aerial service
68. Energizer
69. Moms@work

70. Devita Saraf
71. The Waterbury Clock Company
72. Herbalife International
73. Life Gem
74. Haldirams
75. Karnataka Milk Federation
76. Shanghai Electric Group
77. Golden Rock Locomotive Workshop
78. Dena Bank
79. Coal India
80. Pontiac
81. Pune based Venkateshwara Hatcheries
82. HRH (Historic Resorts Hotels)
83. Ness Technologies
84. Reckitt Benckiser
85. Cadila Health Care
86. Nomura
87. AMD (Advanced Micro Devices)
88. Vestal Enterprise a 100 per cent subsidiary of Vestal Corporation, Singapore
89. Wikileaks
90. Hayes Lemmerz
91. Radico Khaitan
92. Dewan Housing Finance Corporation
93. Hexaware Technologies
94. Grand Bhagwati Group of Hotels and Restaurants
95. Reliance
96. Sundaram Clayton
97. Landmark
98. INQ
99. Shriram Transport Finance Company
100. Landmark
101. Amrutanjan
102. Cable and Wireless (C&W)
103. Lehman Brothers Investment Bank

104. Oil spill at the company's Macondo project deep-water rig in the Gulf of Mexico
105. www.careerstrokes.com
106. Purdue Pharma
107. SABMiller
108. There were only three spaces left after the word Pizza
109. Ladybird
110. Southern Spice Music
111. Dentsu India
112. MMTC Ltd.
113. S. Kumars Nationwide through SKNL North America
114. Manganese Ore India Ltd.
115. Gucci
116. Bottega Veneta
117. Prestige
118. In & Out
119. Bangda airport in Eastern Tibet
120. Reliance Khazana in 1986
121. Taj
122. Alternative Fuels and Raw Materials. Coprocessing is the practice of substituting fossil fuel (mostly coal) with hazardous and other wastes in a cement kiln. The process is referred to as thermal substitution and is considered a better way to dispose of hazardous waste compared to a land fill.
123. Reckitt Benckiser
124. Qantas
125. Berger
126. They started the privately owned management consulting firm Monitor group
127. TT Ltd., (formerly Tirupati Texnit Ltd.) in 1990
128. Schwing Stetter
129. Shri Mahila SEWA Sahkari Bank set-up as an urban cooperative bank
130. The Netherlands. It's usually abbreviated as KLM
131. Nakheel
132. Mahamaza.com
133. D-Link
134. Indian Tobacco Company (since 1970)

135. SoCal
136. A play area where parents can drop their children while they do their shopping
137. Boots
138. Steinway musical instruments. It has chosen LVB to honour composer Ludwig van Beethoven.
139. Seagate Technology
140. Anaconda Copper Mining Company
141. USA. In USA alone Kit Kat is produced under license by The Hershey Company, due to a prior licensing agreement with Rowntree
142. A breed of dog as logo or appears in their advertisement
143. HCL
144. Candico India
145. Shree Cement
146. Maitree
147. Pepperidge Farm
148. Eastman Kodak
149. Burberry
150. Moet & Chandon
151. Tanishq
152. Philips Morris Companies
153. Silk Air
154. Power Corporation of Canada
155. Cost of Goods Sold and Days Inventory Outstanding
156. Ontario Syncrude
157. Genpact
158. Walchand Hirachand (Doshi)
159. In honour of Charles Goodyear who invented vulcanized rubber in 1839
160. Yubiwa pipe, a finger ring that would hold a cigarette allowing the holder to smoke the cigarette down to its nub
161. Trishul
162. 'Leave luck to heaven'
163. China Unicom
164. BIC Corporation
165. *Times of India*
166. Singapore Stock Exchange

167. Karuturi Global Limited and its Managing Director is Ramakrishna Karuturi
168. Hans Wilsdorf
169. The spirit of Sandvik
170. Alpha Moscon Technologies. It was designed to attract mosquitoes using its natural hunting patterns
171. Nikka
172. Barnes and Noble
173. United Airlines
174. Allahabad Bank
175. The Chocolate Tasting Club
176. ITC Royal Gardenia, Bangalore
177. Furtados
178. Facebook
179. The Pune based Kirloskar Foundation
180. Mitsubishi Pencil Company
181. Britannia
182. Reynolds
183. Philips
184. Bacardi
185. Hindustan Pencils (which has brands such as Apsara and Nataraj)
186. Electric Storage Battery Company
187. La Boulangerie
188. National Biscuit Company for its UNEEDA Biscuit
189. Anheuser-Busch
190. SKF
191. Aviva
192. Jockey
193. Rents designer handbags to women. It charges a monthly fee to borrow designer bags which are shipped by FedEx and come with a return shipping label.
194. BNP Paribas
195. Transcend
196. Dell
197. Sahara India Life Insurance
198. WOW (Wealth Out of Waste)
199. Maruti Udyog Ltd.

200. SmithKline Beecham
201. Quality Service and Cleanliness
202. Digital Twin-Spark-Ignition Technology
203. Blaupunkt
204. Punjab National Bank
205. Kamani Tubes Ltd.
206. Tissot
207. Taco Bell
208. Sharp
209. Credila (HDFC now owns a 62 per cent stake in it)
210. Mahindra and Mahindra Group
211. Piperline
212. HUL with Pureit (works without running water or power, gets switched off when not in use and provide germ kill)
213. Vortex Engineering in collaboration with IIT, Madras
214. Parveen Travels, a Chennai-based fleet operator
215. Caran D' Ache
216. IBM
217. Toyota
218. Mahanagar Telephone Nigam Limited, New Delhi is the first Mobile operator in India to launch 3G services named "MTNL 3G Jadoo".
219. Canali; Paolo Canali, MD (3rd generation of the family); founded by the brothers Giovanni and Giacomo Canali
220. Arvind Mills Ltd.
221. PricewaterhouseCoopers LLP
222. LG – abbreviation of 'Lucky Goldstar' but associated with the tagline 'Life's Good'
223. SpiceJet Ltd.
224. Marico Industries
225. Serco
226. Pasha Ventures

❀ ❀ ❀

Questions

1. Which IT training institute was established in 1996 by Atul and Rajesh Nissar?
2. Name the famous online website, a subsidiary of Google created by three former PayPal employees – Chad Hurley, Steve Chen and Jawed Karim in February 2005.
3. Which former Scotland international rugby player founded Cairn Energy?
4. Who founded RCI International and invented an industry by launching the concept of time-share holidays?
5. Who founded the Indian stock broking firm India Bulls Financial Services Limited?
6. Who is the founder of Amazon.com?
7. Who founded TechTribe.com a professional social networking site targeted specifically at IT professionals?
8. Who is the founder of Indian School of Business in Hyderabad as also the Public Health Foundation of India?
9. Which company was started by Shantanu Prakash, India's first K-12 education technology company started with a long-term vision of transforming the teaching learning process by leveraging technology?
10. Hot Mail one of the first web based e-mail services was founded by _________.
11. Which company was founded by Bharat Desai along with his wife Neerja Sethi while as students with a $ 2,000 capital and which has at present more than 13,600 employees?
12. Who is often referred to as the 'Sultan of Sound' and is the founder of a company in his name, its annual sales estimated at $ 2.5 billion?

13. Who is this renowned venture capitalist and co-founder of Sun Microsystem where he stayed as CEO and Chairman in the early 1980s?
14. What is the company established by John Forbes from Scotland, this being India's oldest company and is now part of Shapoorji Pallonji Group?
15. Who is the founder of the Good Year Tyre and Rubber Company?
16. What was founded by the Chicago physician Wallace Calvin in 1888?
17. Which pharma company was founded in 1913 by 400 doctors and pharmacists (apothecaries) in Sweden?
18. JCB the company famous for its Backhoe loaders, excavators and hydraulic tractors was founded by ________.
19. Who was the founder of South West Airlines?
20. Who started the Four Seasons after being inspired by a motel that he himself designed for a family friend?
21. Who is the founder of 'The Body Shop', a cosmetics company producing and retailing beauty products that shaped ethical consumerism?
22. Who founded the Heritage Group in 1992 which at present has three divisions namely dairy, retail and agri?
23. Who founded the Zynga Game network, makers of Facebook games such as Farmville and Mafia wars?
24. In 1939 Walchand Hirachand founded a car company with support from M. Visweswarayya, dewan and architect of Mysore state that was called.
25. Which motor car company was founded by James Ward his brother William Doud and their partner George Lewis Weiss?
26. Who was the former Google engineer who set-up the social networking site Orkut?
27. Vivek Paul's first entrepreneurial venture a corporate social networking solution company which helps every company to set-up its own official equivalent of Facebook for its employees is called ________.
28. Tom's of Maine a leading maker of Natural toothpaste was founded in 1970 by ________.
29. Who originally launched SAB TV in 2000?
30. Who was the inventor of the motel, having started the first one in 1925, The Milestone motel in California?
31. Which cosmetics company was founded by Jonas af Jochnick and Robert af Jochnick?

32. Who started Lotte one of the largest food and shopping groups in Japan and South Korea?
33. Which beer company was started by two American brothers William and Ralph, who owned a refrigeration plant in Melbourne in 1886?
34. Who is the founder of Tempur-Pedic the manufacturers of memory foam mattresses and for which NASA has provided the certified technology seal?
35. Who has introduced the Tempur brand of pillows and mattresses in India in 2008?
36. What was patented by Dr. Robert Hutson a California based periodontist in 1950?
37. Who was the founder of Cadillac?
38. Charles Kettering and Edwards A. Deeds were co-workers at National Cash Register Company. In 1908 Deeds started work on a car he was building from a kit for which Kettering developed a high energy spark ignition system far superior to the weak spark model supplied with the kit. This company was formed when Henry Leland of Cadillac placed an order for five thousand of those ignition sets. Identify the company ________.
39. Maharaja Sayajirao Gaekwad III, wanted to build a modern banking system in his state. On 18 July, 1908 which was considered auspicious as astrologers had predicted that eight planets would come together in a mathematical configuration, he took an elephant ride to a small rented office in the heart of the city and deposited a silver plate filled with 101 gold coins which happened to be the banks first deposit. In 1963 the bank acquired Hind Bank and New Citizen Bank. In 1996 when the divestment process began this became the first Indian Bank to go public. Identify the bank ________.
40. Who founded the Business Intelligence (BI) start-up, SAS, in 1976?
41. Which company was originally founded by Virginio Tedeschi in Turin and is owned by R.P. Goenka Group since 1982?
42. What was invented in 1942 by Dr. Harry Coover and Fred Joyner of Kodak Laboratories during experiments to make a transparent plastic?
43. Who invented gabardine, a hardwearing, water-resistant, breathable fabric, in which the yarn is waterproofed before weaving?
44. Which company started the concept of cause marketing and used money generated from campaigns towards the Statue of Liberty Restoration Project?
45. Who is credited with inventing the "in-sink" food waste disposal in 1927, which works by grinding and shredding solid food waste and founding the company InSinkErator?

46. Who invented Formica while working at Westinghouse and quit in 1913 to start their venture Formica Products Company?
47. What is the name of the hook and loop fastener invented by George De Mestral?
48. Why did George W. Cole name the product that he invented as 3 in 1 oil?
49. Who was the founder of NBC and is credited with a law in his name which states that the value of a broadcast network is proportional to the number of viewers?
50. Super Cassettes Industries Limited (T Series) was established by ________.
51. Who set-up Tehelka.com which was behind the Armsgate scandal?
52. Polaroid Corporation famous for its instant cameras was founded in 1937 by ________.
53. Which online music file sharing service was created by Shawn Fawning?
54. Digital camera was invented by ________.
55. Who started Samsonite in its earlier name in 1910?
56. Who founded Yahoo?
57. Who started the greeting cards and social expressions selling company ARCHIES?
58. Which two teenagers founded the American Messenger Company?
59. The brand Duracell was introduced in 1964 by the partnership of ________.
60. Three young promoters Dhruv Shringi, Manish Amin and Sabina Chopra left their jobs at e-bookers, Makemytrip.com and travelguru.com to start a company. What is it?
61. Who started the present-day American Tourister in the name American luggage works?
62. Who is the founder and CEO of the online gaming company Games2win.com?
63. What was the invention of David Misell that he assigned to the American Electrical Novelty and Manufacturing Company, (the company was later called Eveready)?
64. Hugh Hefner and his associates started a men's magazine part funded by a $ 1,000 loan from Hefner's mother. The magazine is named ________.
65. Which Indian men magazine was started in 1971 by Ashok Row Kavi and Anthony Van Braband?

66. One of India's biggest free SMS service providers 160 by 2 was founded by ________.
67. Who launched sulekha.com a selective online community where all kinds of products and services, *viz.*, furniture, electricians, plumbers, addresses for local businesses and agencies offering maids are on offer?
68. Who established the Le Meridien Hotel to provide a home-away-from-home for its customers?
69. Which airline based in Utah was started by Morris and David Neeleman?
70. Who launched the Mecca Cola in France?
71. Dietrich Mateschitz and Chaleo Yoovidhya owner of TC Pharmaceutical founded a company to adopt Krating Daeng for the European market. Which energy drink are we talking about?
72. Who founded the Twitter organization?
73. Dow Chemical was founded in 1897 by a Canadian born chemist named ________.
74. Who started the Mysore Paints & Varnish Ltd. which was taken over by the state in 1947?
75. Who at the age of 16 along with his brothers Rollie and William founded the Norfolk Post Card Company?
76. Who has promoted India's first aerospace SEZ?
77. Who was the founder of De Beers?
78. The *Washington Post* was founded in 1877 by ________.
79. What was invented by Earl Dickson an employee of Johnson and Johnson for his wife Josephine Dickson who often got injured while doing her cooking?
80. Coca-Cola was invented in the late 19th Century by ________.
81. Who is the founder of Pilot Pen Company?
82. Who founded the Tetra Pak a world leader in liquid food packaging?
83. Which company was started by Alexander MacRae in Sydney, Australia?
84. Who founded Godiva a high end Belgian chocolate maker and named after the legendary Lady Godiva?
85. Who launched Alibaba.com, an e-commerce portal?
86. Who is the founder of Wahaba, a beverage group?
87. Who started Nirma as a one man outfit in Nirma?
88. Who founded Exide in 1888?
89. Who started Consim Info Pvt. Ltd. which houses brands like Bharat matrimony.com, clickjobs.com, Indiaproperty.com?

90. Android and Danger were cofounded by ________.
91. Which lodging chain was started by Chicago restaurateur Marion W. Isbell in 1954?
92. Which company was started by Amit Jaiswal that successfully launched beer brands like Ikon and Target?
93. Which company was founded by Dr. Eli Harari, an Israeli engineer and Sanjay Mehrotra that designs and manufactures flash memory card products?
94. Which British fashion house specializing in luxury shoes and designer bags was founded by Vogue accessories editor Tamara Mellon along with a couture shoe designer?
95. Which company was founded by Peter Shu which counts among its first product, 'JetMate' a laser printer driver?
96. Which American health care company was founded in 1931 by a medical doctor, Davis Baxter as a manufacturer and distributor of intravenous therapy solutions?
97. Who created the brand Bisleri in the year 1965?
98. Who started Garavi Gujarat in 1968, the best selling magazine in UK for the Asian community?
99. Which sportswear brand was started by tennis playing brothers Rajesh Batra and Rajiv Batra?
100. Which chain of fast food restaurants featuring the 'bun halves logo' was started by James McLamore and David Edgerton?
101. What was started in 1922 by a group of six telecom companies, *viz.*, Marconi Radio Communication Company, Metropolitan Vickers, General Electric, Western Electric and British Thomson Houston to broadcast experimental radio service and this company happens to be the world's first national broadcasting organization?
102. Who invented the first dispensable camera in 1986?
103. Who created Tom & Jerry?
104. Who is the founder of Nirvana films?
105. Which company pioneered the introduction of High speed trains?
106. Which American Internet Company is the creator of the virtual world Second Life?
107. Who invented e-mail and designed the @ symbol for the address?
108. Which company was founded by Larry Ellison, Bob Miner and Ed Oates?
109. Who is the developer of Linux Operating Systems?
110. Who were the founders of Sony Corporation?
111. Which IT training institute was established in 1996 by Atul and Rajesh Nissar?

112. Which company was founded in 1968 by Gordon E. Moore and Robert Novce after they left Fairchild Semiconductor?
113. Which company was founded by Mario and his brother Martino in 1913 in Milan?
114. Who invented the lock stitch sewing machine?

Answers

1. Aptech
2. You Tube
3. Sir Bill Gammel in 1980
4. Christel DeHaan
5. Sameer Gehlaut, Saurabh Mittal and Rajiv Rattan all alumni of IIT, Delhi
6. Jeff Bezos
7. Rohit Agarwal
8. Rajat Gupta
9. Educomp
10. Sabeer Bhatia and Jack Smith
11. Syntel
12. Amar Bose of Bose Corporation
13. Vinod Khosla
14. Forbes & Co.
15. Frank Seiberling
16. Abbott Laboratories
17. Astra AB
18. Joseph Cyril Bamford
19. Herb Kelleher and Rollin King
20. Isadore Sharp
21. Dame Anita Roddick
22. Chandrababu Naidu former Andhra Chief Minister
23. Mark Pincus. (Zynga is the hottest start-up to emerge from Silicon valley since Twitter and Facebook)
24. Premier Automobiles Ltd.
25. Packard Motor Car Company in 1899
26. Orkut Buyukkokten
27. Kinetic Glue
28. Tom Chappell

29. Sri Adhikari Brothers
30. Arthur S. Heineman
31. Oriflame
32. Shin Kyuk Ho also known as Takeo Shigemitsu
33. Fosters
34. Bob Trussell
35. Springwel Mattresses Pvt. Ltd.
36. Oral–B toothbrush
37. Henry Leland
38. Delco
39. Bank of Baroda
40. Dr. James Goodnight
41. Ceat
42. Cyanoacrylates (Generic name for fast acting adhesive such as superglue)
43. Burberry
44. American Express
45. John W. Hammes
46. Daniel J. O'Conor and Herbert A. Faber
47. Velcro
48. Because of its triple ability to clean lubricate and protect
49. David Sarnoff
50. Gulshan Kumar
51. Tarun Tejpal
52. Edwin H. Land
53. Napster
54. Steven Sasson, an electric engineer with Eastman Kodak
55. Jesse Shwayder started it as Shwayder trunk manufacturing company
56. Jerry Yang and David Filo in January 1994, Electrical Engineering graduate students at Stanford University
57. Anil Moolchandani
58. Nineteen-year-old Jim Casey and Eighteen-year-old Claude Ryan
59. Samuel Ruben and Philip Roger Mallory
60. Yatra.com
61. Sol Koffler
62. Alok Kejriwal

63. Electric Torch
64. *Playboy*
65. Debonair
66. Satyakalyan Yerramsetti
67. Satya Prabhakar
68. Air France
69. Moris Air
70. Tunisian born French citizen Tawfik Mathlouthi
71. Red Bull energy drink
72. Jack Dorsey
73. Herbert Henry
74. Nalwadi Krishnaraja Wadiyar, the ruler of the then princely state of Mysore
75. Joyce C. Hal
76. Arvind Melligeri of QUEST GLOBAL, the Belgaum based SEZ would churn out aerospace related business worth around ₹ 2,000 crore
77. Cecil Rhodes
78. Stilson Hutchins
79. Band Aid
80. John Pemberton
81. Ryosuke Namik
82. Ruben Rausing
83. McRae knitting mills which is the present-day brand of Speedo swim wear
84. Joseph Draps in Brussels in 1926
85. Jack Ma
86. Zong Qinghou. In rural China, Wahaba's future cola is the market leader
87. Karsanbhai Patel
88. W.W. Gibbs
89. Murugavel Janakiraman
90. Andy Rubin
91. Ramada
92. Manav Breweries
93. SanDisk Corporation
94. Jimmy Choo
95. Transcend
96. Baxter International

97. Signore Felice Bisleri
98. Ramniklal Solanki
99. Proline
100. Burger King
101. British Broadcasting Corporation
102. Fiji film
103. William Hanna and Joseph Barbara
104. Prakash Verma
105. Shinkansen bullet trains, first connected Tokyo and Osaka on 1st October, 1964.
106. Linden Labs launched on June 23, 2003
107. Ray Tomlinson
108. Oracle Corporation
109. Linus Torvaldis
110. Akio Morita and Masaru Ibuka
111. Aptech
112. Intel
113. Prada
114. Walter Hunt in 1833

Questions

1. Marlboro, the largest selling brand of cigarettes in the world is so named after ________.
2. What is the name of the service from HP that allows one to create a magazine or flyer in the PDF format and as and when you order a copy the service will mail and even deliver the magazine to its subscribers?
3. What is the name of the independent sales force created as part of Jockey's direct selling division Jockey Person-to-Person?
4. What is the present name of the company that was originally started as Coopers Inc. by Samuel T. Cooper in 1876 as a hosiery business?
5. Under what name was the present Yamaha company established in 1887 by Torakusu Yamaha?
6. What is the present name of the company known as Matsuhita Electric Industrial Co., founded in 1918 by Konosuke Matsuhita?
7. What was the name of the company that was established by Walchand Hirachand and which was nationalized to become Hindustan Shipyard Ltd.?
8. What is the present name of the company that was incorporated in 1944 as The Boots Company (India) Limited?
9. What is the present name of the company that was formerly named Grisoft, it was a privately held Czech company, formed in 1991 by Jan Gritzbach and Tomas Hofer?
10. This hotel was known as 'The St. James's Club' and 'The Argyle' at different times and was originally designed by Leland A. Bryant and located in West Hollywood. Identify its present name.
11. What is the present name of the company formerly known as Minnesota Mining and Manufacturing Company?
12. What is the present name of the company founded as Swallow Side Car Company by Sir William Lyons in 1922?

13. What is the present name of the company that was started as Rodier mill?
14. What is the name of the company started by Clelia Angelon whose first product was Henna powder formulated with raw materials imported from India?
15. What is the name of the chain of shops founded by Paul Orfalea which provided full service copy and print, fax machines, digital photo printer kiosks and several desktop computer rentals and which is at present being owned by FedEx?
16. What is the present name of the company that was started in 1855 as Asia's first brewery by Edward Dyer at Kasauli in the Himalayas?
17. What is the present name of the company that in its early avatars was the International Time Recording Company, Computing Scale Company and the Computing-Tabulating-Recording Company (CTR)?
18. What is the present name of the company that was founded in 1930 by Marcel Bloch as Societe des Avions Marcel Bloch?
19. What is the present name of the company that grew out of a trading company started by Morimura brothers and later called Nippon Toki Kaisha Ltd.?
20. What is the present name of American Messenger Company?
21. *Femina* is a fortnightly magazine published in India by *The Times* Group since 1959. Femina is a Latin noun meaning _________.
22. Brook Bond was founded by Arthur Brooke who opened his first tea shop in 1869. How did the 'Bond' get included?
23. What is the name under which the drinks that are made in Former Bacardi Distillery sold in Cuba (where Bacardi family had migrated at the beginning of their operation)?
24. Which airline services was started under the name Fairinc?
25. What is the trade name other than Revatio of Sildenafil Citrate being marketed by Pfizer Pharmaceutical Company?
26. Curtis came up with an idea to make and sell spruce gum as chewing gum. Under what name did he market his first batch of chewing gum?
27. What is the name of Michelin tyres signature sustainable mobility event initiated in 1998?
28. What is the present name of the company that was incorporated as Rodio Hazrat & Co. in 1959?
29. What does the meaning of the word ISUZU in Isuzu motor mean?
30. Which brand name of a soap is a palindrome?
31. What was the original brand name in which Konica film and paper was sold?

32. What was the name given to the eight Boeing 737 planes which Jet Airways modified by removing business class seats and instead adding a few more rows of economy, converting the 140 odd seat aircraft to 175 seaters?
33. What was the original name of 7 Up?
34. What is the name of the equivalent to Mach 3 razors being marketed for women by Gillette?
35. What is the original name of Kit Kat?
36. What is the present name of Huafu pen factory founded in 1931?
37. Ssang Yong is Korea's fourth largest automobile manufacturer. What does Ssang Yong mean?
38. What is the inspiration behind Radisson hotel to be named so?
39. From what was the name Exide derived?
40. What is the present name of the company that was started as Kullagerfabriken AB in 1909?
41. What is the name of the company that was started as Minnesota Mining and Manufacturing Company?
42. What is the present name of the product originally called Peutronics Financial Accounting when launched in 1987?
43. How did Nokia get its name?
44. What is the present name of the company that was started as Yasui Sewing Machine Coin 1908 and is at present a diversified Japanese Company involved in the manufacture of printers, fax machines, typewriters, label printers, sewing machines, etc?
45. The Ovaltine known today was exported to England in 1909 as Ovomaltine. Why the name was changed so?
46. Which bath fittings company has been renamed Benelave?
47. What is the present name of the company registered in 1984 by a Houston born man as 'PCs Limited' to sell personal computers directly to consumers, saving the costs of an indirect retail channel?
48. What was Accenture previously known as?
49. Why was the Blaupunkt Company so named?
50. What is the present name of the company Kerala Chemicals & Proteins Limited promoted by Kerala State Industrial Development Corporation to manufacture gelatin, collagen peptide whose name was changed in 2008 to reflect its Japanese collaborator's global standards and values?
51. What is the name of the subsidiary of electronic trading pioneer Instinet, whose name was derived from the 22nd letter of the Greek alphabet, "X" (Chi), symbolizing the "crossing", or matching, of the

two sides of a trade and matched with the "X" from the English alphabet?

52. What is the earlier name of Indage Vintners?
53. Which company was formerly known as IT Microsystems (India) Limited (ITMIL)?
54. Name the subsidiary of Hindustan Construction Company (HCC) Ltd. that is labelled as India's first planned Hill city ________.
55. What is the present name of the web-browser Phoenix?
56. What is the present name of the low-cost airline Air Deccan?
57. This company was started in Lahore as Radio Lamps by Kishanchand Kaycee. During World War II as he could not import glass shells he started a company Kaycee Glass Works for glass shells in Shikohabad. After partition the company was shifted to Jalandhar. He entered into collaboration with Philips Netherland and three leading British electrical firms and renamed the company as Hind Lamps Ltd. In 1954 due to old-age he transferred active management to Kamalnayan. Identify the present name of the company ________.
58. How did Vespa scooter get its name?
59. Which company named after the founder's daughter had its first product called Ujala?
60. Why was Cadillac so named?
61. How did Lambretta scooter get its name?
62. How did Samsonite get its name?
63. What was renamed as Yahoo?
64. Who coined the name LEGO?
65. The name of a moisturizing cream was derived from a Latin word meaning snow. What is it?

Answers

1. Great Marlborough Street, the location of its original London factory
2. MagCloud
3. Comfort specialist consultants
4. Jockey
5. Nippon Gakki Company, Limited
6. Panasonic Corporation
7. The Scindia Shipyard
8. Abbott India Limited
9. AVG Technologies

10. Sunset Tower
11. 3M
12. Jaguar
13. Anglo French Textiles Limited
14. Surya Brasil
15. Kinko
16. Mohan Meakin
17. IBM
18. Dassault Aviation
19. Noritake
20. United Parcel Service
21. Woman
22. Arthur Brooke chose the name simply because it sounded pleasing to his ears
23. Caney
24. Ibex Airlines
25. Viagra
26. State of Maine Pure Spruce Gum
27. Challenge Bibendum
28. AFCONS (Asia Foundations and Constructions Limited now part of Shapoorji Pallonji group)
29. Fifty bells pealing in harmony and celebration
30. Liril
31. Sakura meaning Cherry Blossom in English
32. Konnect
33. Bib – Label Lithiated Lemon – Lime Soda
34. Venus. The Venus models feature different grip shapes and lengths than their Mach 3 counterparts
35. Rowntree's chocolate crisp
36. The Shanghai Hero pen company makers of Hero fountain pens
37. Double Dragon
38. After 17th Century French explorer Pierre-Esprit Radisson
39. Excellent Oxide
40. AB SKF
41. 3M
42. Tally

43. Idestam, the founder built his second plant near the town of Nokia which got its name for Nokianvirta river which flowed through the town and again the river got its name from a dark furred animal that lived on its banks.
44. Brother Industries
45. A misspelling in the trademark registration led to its name being truncate to Ovaltine
46. Crabtree
47. Dell
48. Anderson Consulting
49. The word in Germany means blue dot and named after the blue dot painted on the head phones once it had passed the quality control
50. Nitta Gelatin India Limited.
51. Chi-X
52. Champagne Indage
53. Panoramic Universal, Mumbai-based company
54. Lavasa Corporation
55. Mozilla Firefox
56. Kingfisher Red
57. Bajaj Electricals
58. It refers to wasp in Italian, derived from the high pitched noise of the two-stroke engine and also a reference to its body shape
59. Jyothy Laboratories
60. After the 17th Century French explorer Antoine Laumet de la Mothe, Sieur de Cadillac, who founded Detroit in 1701
61. From a small river Lambro in Milan which flowed near the scooter factory
62. Shwayder named one of his initial cases after the biblical strong man Samson
63. Jerry and David's guide to the world wide web
64. Christiansen from the Danish phrase leg godt, which means "play well"
65. Nivea

✿ ✿ ✿

Questions

1. The Gran Vals composition is that of a Spanish musician of the Romanic Period whose eyesight was permanently impaired in childhood. This tune is well known today as ________.
2. Which company's first product was 'Universalwaschmittel' a detergent based on Silicate?
3. Vivaha Silk is an in-shop brand of ________.
4. What does the SG associated with cricket bats and cricket accessories in India stand for (a French word meaning 'without parallel')?
5. With which brand are the confectionery brands, *viz.*, Mintrox, Buttercup, Buttercup softease and Frewt Eclairs associated with?
6. Which car brand has used the number 9 in their model number in all their models other than one model which was a re-badged Lancia Delta?
7. What is the present name of the company that was originally known as Standard oil of California?
8. Which company markets Equal, a brand of artificial sweetener?
9. Which is the largest India based social networking site in the country?
10. To what name has the lantern that Eveready had branded Homelite changed to?
11. Connect the following mineral water brands to an umbrella group – Evian, Volvic, Badoit, Aqua, Naya, Lanjaron ________.
12. Which biscuit brand invented Sando and Big pie?
13. Which company was acquired by Reckitt Benckiser that enabled it to add OTC brands such as D'Cold, Moov, DermiCool, Krack and Itch Guard and Ring Guard to its portfolio?
14. Which is Asia's first beer brand?

15. Which apparel brand uses the spinnaker logo as a symbol of 'adventure and action' that reflects mass exploration of the world by taking to the sea?
16. Which Indian company came out with advertisement welcoming American president Barrack Obama indicating that they were his tailors with the tagline, 'made in USA, powered by India'?
17. Which Swiss watch brand has launched its latest Septagraph complication watch model inspired by Indian philosophy, indicating the Rahu Kaal period every single day?
18. What is the name of the tobacco cessation product – a sugar free nicotine gum that helps reduce nicotine cravings that is to be launched by Johnson & Johnson?
19. Which company is behind the Iris brand of home fragrances?
20. With which fashion brand does US Polo had a litigation because of which it carries a clear disclaimer that it is not affiliated with that company and to distinguish the two brands?
21. What is the brand name of Axe in UK, Australia and New Zealand?
22. Which brand of wine is known for its centaur logo and called 'man-headed horse' in China instead of its name?
23. Which company has launched the tablet computer Playbook catering to the business class?
24. What is the name of Micromax's lifestyle phone for which another company that manufactures high end mobile phones under the name Movil has taken to court claiming trademark violation?
25. Which company has created the 'Fa Fresh Zone' at a theatre complex in Chennai?
26. Who acquired Eight o'clock Coffee in 2005, the brand having been started in 1859 by American supermarket chain A&P?
27. Which is the world's first glue stick, released by Henkel in 1969?
28. Which company launched the Gold Coin apple juice?
29. Which company's first product was 'Backin', a pre-measured amount of baking powder that when mixed with requisite amount of flour and other ingredients produce a cake?
30. Which company introduced Sunny Tonny Range of cricket bats endorsed by Little Master Sunil Manohar Gavaskar?
31. What is the name of the shampoo variant that Sunsilk from Hindustan Lever launched by tying up with world renowned stylist Jamal Hammadi?
32. What is the reason for a brand of hydrogenated vegetable oil to be called as Dalda?

33. What is the brand name of the edible oil brand of Emami Group?
34. L&T cement has since 2004 been rebranded as _________.
35. Indian Furniture Products Ltd. pioneered the concept of ready to assemble furniture in India and set-up a chain of Gautier stores. After seven years when their contract with Gautier ended, they decided to go solo. What is their present brand name?
36. What is the present name of the company that was earlier called the Arabian American Oil Company (ARAMCO)?
37. How did IKEA, the Dutch Corporation that designs and sells ready to assemble furniture, appliances and home accessories get its name?
38. Kahuna, Blade and Ice are brands associated with _________.
39. What is the name of the safe and healthy alternative to tobacco, the 'tobacco free bidi' which stimulates the pleasure of tobacco and mimics the kick without the ills associated with tobacco developed from Indian plants by Dalmia Consumer Care?
40. Which is the world's largest selling household food waste disposer?
41. What is the name of the line of deodorants and perfumes for men and women that MTV launched through a tie-up with Scion International; a Dubai based global lifestyle and beauty solutions company?
42. Discovery Travel and Living, the lifestyle entertainment channel has been rebranded as _________.
43. Which Indian hospitality chain's indigenous spa brand is Kayakalp?
44. What is the name of the stove that BP Energy co-created with villagers and for which the NGO's Swayam Shikshan Prayog and Covenant Centre for Development formed Adharam Energy which happens to be the BP's exclusive in selling the stove?
45. What is the name of the tile and stone system introduced by Pidlite Industries for applications like tile-on-tile, waterproofing of areas before tiling, tile joint filler, stoner sealer, etc., that makes tile fixing less time-consuming and hassle free?
46. If three roses is to tea, what is four roses?
47. Which is the world's largest handheld computer manufacturer and whose brands include Treo 600 and Tungsten T5?
48. Who founded Dilma, a brand of Ceylon tea which was also the sponsor of Sri Lankan cricket team from 2001 to 2008?
49. Which brand name was coined by a London student Herbert Grime in a national competition set by S. Fitton & Sons Ltd. to find a trading name for their patent flour, the meaning of the word from Latin means 'strength of man'?

50. Who created the concept of serviced apartments with his Oakwood apartments brand and ensured travellers had a spacious alternative to staying in a hotel room?
51. What is the name of the brand of premium cigar manufactured by Cuban state-owned Tobacco Company and which was originally a private brand supplied exclusively to Fidel Castro and high-level officials in the Communist Party of Cuba?
52. Which company is credited with creating the designer jean market through the invention of stretch jeans?
53. What is the DuPont trade name for its brand of poly chloroprene (synthetic rubber produced by polymerisation of Chloroprene)?
54. What is the proposed name of the e-book reader to be introduced by Sharp?
55. If Seven o'clock is to blade, what is Eight o'clock?
56. What is the name of the chain of coffee shops started by Amalgamated Bean Coffee Trading Company Ltd.?
57. In 1932, *Johnie Walker* Swing was launched, the name arising from _________.
58. Konica SLR interchangeable lenses were named _________.
59. What was the original name of *Johny Walker* whisky?
60. Jacob Davis a tailor who started making men's work pants with metal points for greater strength joined with Lob Straub (original name) to make a famous product. What is it?
61. Cashmere Bouquet a perfumed soap was introduced in 1872 by _________.
62. Which renowned manufacturer of microscopes has named its company after the home of the twelve supreme Gods and Goddesses of Greek mythology?
63. Connect Speaking Tree, Crest, View from Venus, Life and Culture curry to an Indian brand _________.
64. What is the name of the first bag designed for Hidesign by Italian Alberto Ciaschini?
65. Which publishing group has started Manila, an entity focused on digital management of household bills and accounts?
66. *Fortune, Force 10,* Senorita, Warrior, Windsor are brands associated with _________.
67. What was the name of the firm that Rudolf Dasler formed which was later rebranded as Puma?

68. Coimbatore based Jaganath Textiles Company is opening exclusive outlets to sell its men's innerwear product under the brand name ________.
69. Britannia Industries in the first instance had entered the flavoured milk business some ten years ago and exited quickly under the brand name ________.
70. Who was the first Bollywood star to have a perfume named after her?
71. What is the name of the e-book reader developed by Barnes and Nobles based on the Android platform?
72. What is the name of the software and hardware platform developed by Amazon.com for the rendering and display of e-books and other digital media?
73. Which company has launched a range of herbal hair and skin care products under the brand 'Beauty secrets by Madhuri'?
74. Which company has come up with the F-row initiative, wherein the 'F' row across all the theatres will be branded with the company's name and 'F' row ticketholders would be entitled to special benefits and surprises?
75. Connect Persil detergents, Loctite glue and Schwarzkopf hair products to an Umbrella brand ________.
76. Ketel One vodka was originally started in 1691 by Nolet family in Holland and has passed directly from father to son for ten generations, with the 11th now *firmly* involved. Ketel one is still produced using the same method dating back 300 years. How did the brand get this name?
77. Which Indian corporate head's daughter is Amrita, whose debut Bollywood film is *Aisha* based on Jane Austen's novel *Emma,* in which she plays the second lead a behenji-type who gets turned into a swan by the heroine?
78. Which talent management company has signed Indian cricketer Mahendra Singh Dhoni for ₹ 210 crore making him joint no. 2 in the world in terms of sport players earnings?
79. Which company's trademark are 'Pressman', 'Watchman', 'Discman', 'Talkman' and 'Scoopman'?
80. Ernest Henderson and Robert Moore acquired the Stonehaven Hotel in Massachusetts but their hotel chain was named after a hotel they both acquired earlier which had a lighted name board which was expensive for them to change. Hence it became their brand name. In 1945 it became the first hotel chain to be listed in the New York Stock Exchange. In 1961 they opened their first hotel outside North America in Tel Aviv. Identify the name of this hotel chain –

81. Connect the brands – Kodak, Promax, Taral, Proviz and I-Viz to an umbrella brand _________.
82. What is the name of the speciality home interior stores run by India's largest sanitaryware maker Hindware?
83. Irshad Mirza of Mirza International Ltd. supplies shoes to top brands in 24 countries in addition to having his own brand which he markets without conflict of interest in some countries and also has 45 stores across the country where apart from shoes he has also introduced apparels and denims under the same brand name. What is his brand?
84. What is the name of the country's first branded sugarcane juice launched by Gopadi Srinivasa Rao, where every stage of the entire process is mechanized?
85. Robert Cade, Dana Shires, Harry James Free, Alejandro de Quesada medical researchers at University of Florida, in 1965 created a thirst quencher called _________.
86. What is the name of the sports drink manufactured by the Coca-Cola company and introduced in 1988?
87. Who established Havana Club, a brand of rum?
88. What is common between Air Mauritius, Aeroflot, British Airways and Air Sahara other than that they have airplane services?
89. Connect the UK based personal care company Keyline, South Africa based companies Rapidol and Kinky, Nigeria based player Tura and Indonesia based household insecticides player Magasari Makmur to an Indian umbrella brand _________.
90. What was created by Charles Leiper Grigg in 1920 that contained Lithium Citrate, a mood stabilizing drug?
91. Forbes brand the branded apparel venture of Shapoorji Pallonji Group has launched T-shirts under the brand name _________.
92. Under what brand name did Blue bells develop a jeans line for cow boys hiring famous tailor Rodeo Ben?
93. Zune is a portable media player made by _________.
94. Kin One and Kin Two were a line of smart phones created by _________.
95. What was developed by a South African chemist named Graham Gordon Wulff that helped military burn victims prevent their skin from getting dehydrated?
96. What is the name of the retail venture started as a brand building exercise of Linc Pens?
97. Which group has forayed into the branded retail jewellery segment with 'Cupid Stores' showcasing a line of exclusive gold and diamond jewellery?

98. Which company released the first ever comprehensive line of DC and marvel action figures coded, 'world's greatest super-heroes'?
99. What is the present name of the company that was started as a ground wood pulp mill by mining engineer Fredrik Idestam in 1865?
100. Which umbrella company comprises businesses like Carrier, Hamilton Sundstrand, Otis, Pratt & Whitney and Sikorsky?
101. What was the brand name of the product when five competing tea companies – Rossel industries, Tata Tea, Williamson Magor, Warrens and Goodricke – came together in the early 90s to market branded tea in Russia?
102. Livin Smart is a range of furniture line introduced by ________.
103. The denim collection of the apparel brand Van Huesen is called ________.
104. Which Johnson & Johnson leading pain killer medicine had to be recalled after unknown suspects tampered the product by injecting it with cyanide after it reached the retailer shelves?
105. Which company owns the Havoline motor oil brand?
106. What is the brand name of the mechnical clock designed by Jean-Léon Reutter and which derives energy from small temperature changes and atmospheric pressure changes in the environment and run without human intervention and manufactured by Jaeger-LeCoultre since 1935?
107. Which Indian product got its brand name from a Leon Delibes opera about an Indian maiden?
108. Which watch company created a nano-crystalline diamond enabling it to create the hardest watch on the earth?
109. What company that also manufactures bikes and cars produces the Kalashnikov series of assault rifles?
110. Name the brand of Contact lenses of Titan Industries ________.
111. Which company owns Yummiez, a frozen food brand and Real Good, a raw chilled chicken brand?
112. Name the first and only holiday brand in India that exclusively caters to the unique needs of the premium traveller and is also the winner of the esteemed 'World's Leading Tour Operator' award for nine years ________.
113. Name India's first premium designer lingere brand ________.
114. Name the luxury multibrand retail chain of GCPL ________.
115. What is the multibranded discounted retail chain launched by Krishna Group (Krishna Lifestyle Technologies Ltd.)?

116. Which brand, when it was developed, was called "Richardson's Group and Pneumonia Cure Salve"?
117. Name the first branded Jewellery of India ________.
118. Which company owns the popular tea brands Lal Ghora and Kala Ghora?
119. Name the company that was supplying products to Bodyshop and after Bodyshop's acquisition by L'Oreal started its campaign on fair trade. It presently promotes itself as an independent ethical green brand from UK that stands for no preservatives and no animal testing ________.
120. Which is the largest FMCG brand in India?
121. D.P. Dandekar started this company as a cottage outfit in Girgaum, Mumbai in 1931, making inks and selling them to nearby schools. While at an Irani Café in Mumbai he chanced upon an advertisement for America's Camel cigarettes – 'I'd walk a mile for a Camel'. This happened to be the inspiration behind the name of his brand. The company has also diversified into pharmaceuticals and fine chemicals. Identify the brand ________.
122. Name the fast food venture of Rasna Pvt. Ltd. ________.
123. Name the for-profit experimental venture started in Rajasthan in partnership with Nithin Nihria of Harvard Business School as a network of tele clinics that recruits and trains local literate women to become sevaks ________.

Answers

1. The Nokia tune
2. Henkel
3. Chennai Silks
4. Sanspareils Greenlands
5. Parle Agro
6. SAAB
7. Chevron Corporation
8. Merisant
9. Ibibo
10. Nulite
11. Danone
12. Crown confectionery
13. Paras Pharmaceuticals
14. Lion beer

15. Nautica
16. SKumars for its Hart Schaffner Marx brand
17. Borgeaud
18. Nicorette
19. Ripple fragrance part of Ranga Rao & Sons Group who markets the Cycle brand of agarbattis
20. Ralph Lauren Polo
21. Lynx
22. Remy Martin
23. Research in Motion
24. Bling
25. Henkel Spic India. At city's Satyam Complex in addition to providing air-conditioned comfort, the various fragrances of Fa deodorants are introduced through air-conditioning ducts.
26. Tata
27. Pritt, that entered the market in 1969
28. Mohan Meakin
29. Dr. Oetker
30. Sanspareils Greenlands
31. Stunning Black Shine
32. It was originally imported from Netherlands by a trading company Dada Limited. When it was acquired by Hindustan Lever and as the trading company still wanted to have its connections Hindustan Lever added an L in between to form Dalda
33. Healthy and Tasty
34. Ultra Tech Cement
35. Style Spa
36. Saudi Arabian Oil Company
37. IK stands for the name of the founder Ingvar Kamprad, E stands for Elmtaryd the farm where he grew up and A stands for Agunnaryd his home parish
38. Kookaburra
39. Vardaan
40. In–Sink–Erator
41. MTV Plugged
42. TLC
43. Welcome Group
44. Oorja

45. Roff
46. Blended whisky from Frankfort Distillers Corporation, NY
47. Palmone
48. Merrill J Fernando
49. Hovis
50. Howard F. Ruby
51. Cohiba
52. Fiorucci
53. Neoprene
54. Galapagos
55. Coffee
56. Café Coffee Day
57. The unusual shape of the bottle which allowed it to rock back and forth
58. Hexanon
59. Walker's Kilmarnock whisky
60. Levi's brand of jeans. They used copper rivets to strengthen the pockets of denim work pants.
61. Colgate
62. Olympus (Based on Mount Olympus)
63. Supplements of *Times of India*
64. Ayesha named after Dilip Kapur's daughter.
65. Hearst
66. The Karnal based Liberty Shoes Limited
67. Ruda
68. Crusoe
69. Zipsip
70. Zeenat Aman
71. Nook
72. Kindle
73. Emami
74. Fosters
75. Henkel
76. It is named after the original, coal fired copper pot still, Distilleer Ketel no. 1 – a Dutch word meaning pot still
77. Aditya Puri, the Managing Director of HDFC Bank
78. Rhiti Sports

79. Sony
80. Sheraton
81. GKB Ophthalmics
82. Evok interior
83. Red Tape
84. Cane–O–La
85. Gatorade
86. Powerade
87. José Arechabala
88. Helicopter Services
89. They are all stand-alone companies which are now subsidiaries of Godrej consumer products
90. 7 Up
91. Campbell
92. Wrangler
93. Microsoft
94. Microsoft
95. Oil of Olay
96. Just Linc
97. Mumbai's 100-year-old Tribhovandas Bhimji of Zaveri Bazar
98. Mego Corporation
99. Nokia
100. United Technologies
101. Nargis
102. Spencers Retail
103. Vdot
104. Tylenol
105. Texaco
106. Atmos
107. Lakme
108. V10K by Rado
109. IZHMASH
110. Titan Eye + (TE+).
111. Godrej Agrovet Limited
112. Kuoni Holidays, launched on Jan. 24th, 2006 as a part of Kuoni, the 100-year-old Switzerland based travel group

113. BWITCH, from Genesis Luxury, a unit of Genesis Colours Pvt. Ltd.
114. Samsaara
115. The Grab Store
116. Vicks Vaporub
117. Gili, Gitanjali Group
118. Dhunseri Petrochem & Tea Ltd.
119. Lush
120. Gold Flake
121. Camlin
122. Devil's Workshop
123. Piramal e-Swasthya

Questions

1. Which diabetes drug, sold globally as 'Avandia' was taken-off market shelves by GlaxoSmithKline, following global reports linking it to an increase in strokes and heart attacks?
2. Which is the world's fastest and most expensive street legal super car sold in India?
3. What is the present name of the tailoring shop New Lord & Company which was acquired by Arjan Daswani who transformed the miniature boutique into a mega shirt store?
4. New York chemist T.L. Williams noticed his sister applying a mixture of coal dust and Vaseline to her eyelashes to give them a darker fuller look. He produced the product in his laboratory and the product's name was based on his sister's name from whom he took the inspiration for the product. Identify the product name ________.
5. What is the name of medium-weight balanced plain-woven fabric made from dyed cotton or cotton-blend yarn which is used as a test fabric while designing fashion?
6. What is the name of the battery-operated ten seater three-wheeler scooter rickshaw launched by Mahindra & Mahindra?
7. What is the name of the computer program developed by Norman H. Nie and C. Hadlai Hull in 1968?
8. XCD 28 and XCD 35 range of smart phones has been launched by ________.
9. Which manufacturer of pet foods recalled 60 million containers of food after animals died during quality control tests where later the contaminants were identified as Melamine and Cyanuric acid?
10. With which group has Pizza Hut entered into a partnership through which it will serve wine in select outlets in India?
11. Which now extinct audio format has got its own museum in the Deep Ellum arts district of Dallas?

12. The entire Daimler India commercial vehicles' portfolio of trucks from 6 to 49 tonnes has been branded
13. Where is the first double end ferry Lots Bridge, operated in India for movement of containers?
14. Which product was developed by Australia based Scottish born William Ramsay and named it as a homage to his wife Annie Elizabeth Meek Ramsay based on her native country?
15. Which chocolate malt which when mixed with milk produces a beverage was developed by Australian Chemist Thomas Mayne?
16. Who produced the world's largest truck by dimension?
17. What is the name of the spherical chocolate made by an Italian chocolate manufacturer whose products include Tic Tac and Nutella which consists of a whole roasted hazelnut encased in a thin wafer shell filled with hazelnut cream and covered in milk chocolate and chopped hazelnuts and walnuts, individually packaged inside a gold-coloured wrapper, the meaning of the name in French is 'rock'?
18. Which industry major launched, 'The Eternity', the world's 'Most forgettable battery', which promises hassle free use as one only needs to install it and can simply forget about it, a total concept of product plus service?
19. This company started-off by making pickle and chemical storage jars at its Ranipet factory in 1952. In 1985, the company launched 'Cascade' touted as India's first water saving closet in collaboration with Swedish IFO Sanitar. The brand position of a bathroom to a glamour room was made with the introduction of new age light weight polymer cistern in 1988. In 1999 it acquire Johnson Peddar and its facilities at Dewas in Madhya Pradesh. The company for the first time in India introduced a single piece closet suite, the Colorado Closet, a water saving six litre flush. Identify the company ________.
20. Which was the first toothbrush to go to the moon, which rode on Apollo-11 missions?
21. Which company introduced Nu Life Chewettes, an over-the-counter product, promoted as a safer alternative to cigarettes and gutka in collaboration with New York based Health Care LLC?
22. HUL's Sewree factory in Mumbai saw prolonged agitation in the 1980s when the company attempted to break the union with a two-year lockout in 1988-89 for which the workers responded by beginning an alternate soap production unit and introduced a detergent brand. What is the name of the detergent?
23. Who acquired Carnation Nutra-Analogue Foods Ltd. in 2006 which manufactured Nutralite, a best selling brand of margarine?

24. What is the reason for Singapore to host the 'Formula One' at night time?
25. A new cultural phenomenon was started when Neil Mapworth and Richard Jarvis shared this thing in December 1992. Identify ________.
26. Which was the first military aircraft to be constructed in India?
27. What was developed by L. Valentine Pulsifer, claimed as the first ever clear varnish?
28. What was designed by Friedrich Fischer in 1883 that served as the basis for the roller-bearing market?
29. Which is considered as the world's first microfinance institution?
30. What is the name of a light weight plain weave cotton cloth used as a fabric for lace and needle work?
31. Which is the world's largest tethered helium balloon?
32. Which watch was named as the world's most functional watch in 1989 by the Guinness Book of records with 21 distinct functions?
33. Why was the name Formica chosen for the composite material?
34. What is Google's OS for smart phones called?
35. The first delivery of Airbus A 380 was taken by ________.
36. What was the name of the first product, a bellows camera turned out by Nichi-Doku (the precursor of Minolta Co., Ltd.)?
37. Which is the world's first camcorder with a zoom lens?
38. What was the first product produced by Matsuhita Electric to be marketed under the brand name National?
39. B.J. Johnson of the 'B.J. Johnson Company' who made a popular soap named it Palmolive because the soap was made entirely of ________.
40. Which lenses were popularized by the American photo journalist David Douglas Duncan at the time of the Korean war?
41. The world's first digital camera to feature a full colour, active matrix Organic Light Emitting Diode (OLED) display was ________.
42. Nintendo founded by Fusajiro Yamauchi initially made ________.
43. Which type of pasta name means little worms in Italian?
44. What does the PET in PET bottles stand for?
45. What is the name of the e-book reader developed by the Polish company Kolporter Info SA?
46. What is called the 'Tin Goose' because of its corrugated metal construction?
47. What was the first product to be introduced by Old Spice?
48. Which was the first toothpaste to be packaged in a collapsible tube?

49. Which popular candy gets its name from a race horse?
50. What is the name of the $ 35 Linux based laptop targeted principally at the education segment flagged-off by HRD Minister Kapil Sibal?
51. Chemical resources started manufacturing herbal drugs and pharmaceuticals intermediaries and in 2003 the company came up with a revolutionary product meant for curing diabetes. What is it?
52. Which is the first electric powered washing machine?
53. Which company has launched 'Diva' a classy light weight tableware?
54. What was the first Japaneese produced end-user camera?
55. Which is the world's most stolen painting?
56. What was manufactured by the present Yamaha Company when it was set-up in 1887?
57. What was the material used in the production of Sheaffer's jade green pen?
58. What is the name of the first mass produced repeating rifle developed by Johan Friedrich in 1869?
59. Boultbee Brooks started selling leather goods through the cobbled streets of Midland from a horse and a cot. When his horse died he replaced it with a new fangled safety bicycle. Which product did he invent that became a worldwide success which was necessitated by the difficulties he encountered because of the bike's wooden saddle and solid tyres?
60. HybrelTM, a first in plating strip steel, a coating that combines properties of both metals and particles and Ymagine, a new generation, light gauge, pickled and oiled steel used in the automotive construction sectors were developed by ________.
61. With whom did Nippon Steel in 2006 create a high tensile strength steel which found application in fabrication of hull of ships and facilitated fuel savings due to lesser thickness?
62. Which company launched the world's first electronic digital watch?
63. This Japanese company set-up in 1912 created the world's first mechanical pencil, transistor radio and black and white television. It has recently entered India with differentiated products such as portable air-conditioners, multisplit inverter AC where a single outdoor compressor unit will cater to three indoor cooling units and a refrigerator code named Butterfly that can be opened either from the left or right. Identify the company________.
64. What is the name of the tablet developed by the Bangalore based Notion Ink Company to compete with Ipad?
65. Name the low cost water purifier of Eureka Forbes launched as a competitor to HCL's Pureit ________.

66. Which company had made a pathbreaking innovation as world's first compact camera with in-built projector?
67. Which company has used the engraved image of Gandhiji for the sale of its limited edition pens to commemorate his 140th birthday?
68. Name the technology that can be set in cameras to capture anything from mild sneers to Cheshire Cat grins (detects best grin and captures it).
69. Who launched the disposable contact lenses in 1995 designed to be worn and disposed of the same day?
70. What is the registered trademark for photo goods?

Answers

1. Windia (Rosiglitazone)
2. Bugatti Veyron 16.4 Grand Sport
3. Charagh Din
4. Maybelline
5. Gingham
6. Bijilee
7. SPSS (Statistical Package for the Social Sciences)
8. Dell
9. Menu Foods Ltd.
10. United Breweries group for four seasons wine
11. The 8-track audio tape/catridge
12. BharatBenz
13. Between Willingdon island and Bolghatty
14. Kiwi
15. Milo
16. Terex 33–19 "Titan"
17. Ferrero Rocher manufactured by Ferrero Spa
18. Exide Industries
19. Parryware
20. Oral-B
21. Ceejay Health Care
22. Lockout
23. Zydus Wellness (Cadilla Health Care)
24. Most Television viewers are in Europe and the time difference suits them

25. The world's first ever short messaging service
26. HF-24 designed by German Engineer, Dr. Kurt Tank
27. Valspar
28. He designed the ball grinder that allowed steel balls in large volumes to be ground to an absolutely round state
29. The Irish Loan Fund (1720)
30. Cambric
31. DHL balloon
32. Astrolabium Galileo Galilei by Ulysse Nardin
33. It acted as a substitute product for the mineral mica which was used at that time for electrical insulation
34. Android
35. Singapore Airlines
36. Nifcarette, in March 1929
37. Reflex Zoom 8
38. Bicycle Lamp
39. Palm and Olive oil
40. Nikon lenses
41. Konica Easy share LS633 Digital camera
42. Hand-made playing cards
43. Vermicelli
44. Polyethylene Terephthalate
45. eClicto
46. Ford 4AT Trimotor, Ford's most successful aircraft
47. Early American Old Spice for women a fragrance introduced in 1937
48. Colgate Ribbon Dental Cream
49. Lollipop
50. Sakshat
51. Fenfuro
52. The Thor, introduced in 1908 by the Hurley Machine Company of Chicago and invented by Alva J. Fischer
53. The Kolkata based La Opala with brand ambassador as Bipasha Basu
54. Cherry Portable Camera sold by Konishi in 1902
55. JACOB III DE GHEYN. It has been snatched and recovered four times in the past 35 years.
56. Piano and Reed organ

57. Radite (trade name for a plastic formed of Pyroxylin a partially nitrated cellulose)
58. Vetterli rifle
59. Brook's saddle
60. Corus
61. Mitsubishi Heavy Industries Limited
62. Pulsar
63. Sharp
64. Adam
65. Aquasure
66. Nikon's Coolpix
67. Montblanc
68. Smile Shutter Technology introduced by Sony.
69. Vistakon
70. AGFA

Questions

1. Who from GE Capital's call centre operations left to establish his own IT enabled services company Spectrmind?
2. Who was the American entrepreneur who owned 1800-Flowers which was one of the first companies to pioneer and popularize the use of toll-free telephone numbers and website to sell goods and services directly to consumers?
3. Who has launched the top end watches brand retail shop Ethos, who earlier established Kamla Dials?
4. In 1882, X made hundred casks of blended whisky and hired experts to taste them. The batch from the vat numbered 69 was adjudged the best and hence this scotch blended whisky was named Vat 69. Identify X ________.
5. Her father Bish Agarwal co-founded ABC Consulting and her husband co-headed Manpower India. Identify this personality who is the CEO of executive search firm Accord ________.
6. Which Indian Group has acquired Britain's leading towel brand Christy?
7. Who was the industry leader who wrote Pepperidge Farm Cookbook in 1963, the first cookbook ever to make the *New York Times* best seller list?
8. Social Network, a Hollywood film is based on the life of ________.
9. He started in 1992 as a perfume exporter. He started his business SFP Sons (India) as a small business in Madras export processing zone. His first product was Ahsan Attarfull. Later he created products like Tara Hair Oil and Tara Talcum Powder created brands like Mallaki, Taibah, Al-Amir, Al-Sultan and Crazy Moments. Identify the personality ________.
10. Bombay Dyeing had tied-up with Sabyasachi and another designer to launch a signature line of bed linen. Identify the designer ________.

11. Who founded the fashion label Zara which has a policy of zero advertising and instead uses a portion of its revenues to open new stores?
12. Who is the co-founder of Facebook and the chief digital organizer for President Barack Obama's presidential campaign, who started www.jumo.com, a site meant for giving?
13. Which Indian company's UK arm recently acquired British Salt?
14. Sir Sorabji Pochkhanawala was working in a British bank. He believed in Indian ability and set-up a 'truly Indian bank' on December 21, 1911. The bank brought a series of firsts, like home savings deposit, safe deposit lockers and an exclusive ladies department way back in 1924. Identify the organization ________.
15. Who in 1989 visualized an internet based medium that would allow people to share information while working by enabling the world's first web server at info.cern.ch setting-off a powerful technological revolution?
16. Which bank has a tie-up with oil marketing company Bharat Petroleum Corporation Limited to provide basic banking facilities for small distance commercial vehicle drivers, auto drivers, conductors, cleaners, etc., through the business correspondent model where it has set-up handheld devices that will enable deposit, withdrawal of cash through smart cards?
17. Who coined the term 'Marketing Myopia' in his 1960 paper that refers to a focus on the product rather than on the customer?
18. Who is the Irish rock star who launched the global brand 'Product Red' with different products including credit cards, sun glasses, T-shirts with corporates including GAP, Nike owned Converse and Giorgio Armani with money from sale of these products channelled into funds for AIDS, TB and Malaria?
19. From 1954 to 1962, Ronald Reagan spent ten weeks each year travelling the country as a brand ambassador of this company. In October 2010, the company released a short film titled "Rendezvous with destiny: Reagan's journey from ________ to the White House". Identify the company ________.
20. He started-off as a bicycle parts maker and started manufacturing telephones in 1985. When the insurance sector opened up he formed a joint venture for both general and life insurance. His firm pioneered the 'outsourcing' model in telecom. He also built India's first telecom MNC after acquiring African giant Zain Telecom and Bangladesh's Warid Telecom besides starting operations in Sri Lanka. Identity this personality.
21. He started with his family owned jute mill and seed trading business at Rajam, Andhra Pradesh. He turned around Vysya Bank, in which

he was a major shareholder. In 1996, he entered the infrastructure sector after obtaining permission to set-up a power plant at Basin bridge. He now has three power plants, three airports and six roads in operation. Identify the personality _________.

22. Who coined the term Intrapreneurship in 1985 which refers to 'free market entrepreneurship within the corporate organization'?
23. Who was the co-founder of Crossword, a book store and later sold-off his shares to Shoppers' Stop to set-up a consultancy, Next Practice Retail?
24. Pizza Hut was started by _________.
25. Who was the former CEO of Madura Garments who set-up Indigo Nation, which competes with Madura Garments?
26. Which popular hair dresser has approached the market to raise ₹ 60 crore which is to be the first entity of its kind to raise money by issuing equity to the public?
27. What was the term coined based on cost reduction exercises carried out on a number of company's products by Lawrence Miles while he was working at General Electric?
28. Who was one of the founding members of Covansys who later started Indigo Technologies and Qwiky's Coffee?
29. Which industrialist credited as a fore-runner of marketing tactics such as direct mail, money-back guarantees, travelling salesmen, self-service, free delivery, buy one get one free and illustrated catalogues designed as part of anti-slavery campaign in 1787 the medallion, 'Am I Not a Man and a Brother'?
30. What is the name of the company that was founded by drummer Jim Marshall that designs and manufactures music amplifiers?
31. Which company has started building India's first Solar photovoltaic equipment manufacturing facility at Rajnandgaon in Chhattisgarh?
32. Who coined the term BRIC in his 2001 paper titled "The world Needs Better Economic BRICS", whose combined GDPs as per Goldman Sachs could exceed that of the largest economies in the world by 2050?
33. Mammen Mapilai started as a balloon maker in 1946 and created his own advertisement which read, 'Buy a balloon and build your child's lungs!' From balloon making he shifted to tyre retreading and then to tyre manufacturing by entering into a collaboration with Mansfield tyre company of the US. He had the foresight to tie-up with American oil major ESSO (now HPCL) for selling tyres through oil company's retail outlets when the TBA (Tyres, Batteries and Accessories) concept was first introduced. Identify the company _________.

34. Who is the student of Louis Pasteur who developed 'Heineken A-Yeast' which still happens to be a key ingredient of Heineken beer?
35. Who at seventeen years of age was hired as Christian Dior's assistant and when Dior died four years later he was named head of the House of Dior?
36. Pulin Shroff whose family drew inspiration from traditional book of medicines to create high quality ayurvedic products joined hands with Novartis for its animal health care products – Hormotone, Livivet and Milchey – a first of its kind ayurvedic – allopathic tie-up. Its brand portfolio includes Livomyn, M2tone, Hyponidd and Kofol. Identify the company ________.
37. Who established Bottega Veneta an Italian luxury goods house in 1966?
38. Who was the founder of Polaris software lab?
39. Who launched a fortnightly in 2004 called *Time Out*, Mumbai?
40. Which company was started by A.G. Krishnamurthy in Ahmedabad with 15 employees with Vimal as its first client and it launched the 'I love you Rasna Campaign' in 1983?
41. Who coined the term 'Management by wandering around'?
42. Who coined the term, 'Transformational leadership'?
43. Who is the founder of Hexaware who also started Aptech computer education in 1984?
44. Who quit Oracle to set-up Siebel systems, which offers e-business applications and services in direct competition to Siebel's old company?
45. Who in 2004 founded a human space flight start up company called Blue Origins?
46. Who created a method to generate original ideas called brain-storming?
47. Which company that specializes on the development and marketing of peptides for use in human medicine was started by Fredrik Paulsen in Malmo, Sweden?
48. Who is the son of a famous ice cream company owner who in his book, *'Diet for a new America'* advocates against the use of dairy products and attributes the death of some of his family members to consumption of ice cream?
49. Bhanubhai Patel launched this company in 1951 which was shifted to Vallabh Vidyanagar in Gujarat after the bifurcation of Bombay state. It operates in the field of material handling equipments gear markets. It also manufactures air operated loaders through a joint venture with US based mining equipment manufacturer EIMCO. Identify the company ________.

50. Who has tied-up with pharmaceutical company Elder Pharma to launch a fairness cream, Fair One?
51. Which fashion accessory was manufactured by Prasad Pabrekar through his unit Span Apparels Pvt. Ltd.?
52. Who has promoted Otarian, a strictly vegetarian fast food chain with outlets in New York and London?
53. What is the present name of the company that was started in 1890 as A.G. Thompson Pvt. Ltd. by Alfred Grace Thompson, a migrant harness and saddle maker?
54. What is the name of the shoe manufacturing company founded by former Adidas senior vice-president Simon Skirrow?
55. Who owns the clothing line JustSweet and Sweetface?
56. Hispano Carrocera SA a large manufacturer of bus and coach cabins in Europe and a fully-owned subsidiary of Tata Motors was started in 1939 by ________.
57. Kunwar Sachdev, son of a low ranked railway employee, after graduation started by providing a helping hand to his brothers writing pen distribution business. In 1992, he set out to assemble and manufacture cable television accessories like dish antenna, modulators, satellite receivers and amplifiers. He also got exclusive rights to distribute products of Echo Star, USA in India. In 1997 he entered into the manufacture of inverters. He also set-up a factory in Baddi, Himachal Pradesh for the manufacture of batteries. Identify his company ________.
58. Which soap was manufactured when Nalvadi Krishnaraja Wodeyar set-up the government soap factory in Bangalore?
59. Varalvar who was working with Shipping Corporation of India, along with his father started a pharma formulation facility. This company is now a leading manufacturer and exporter of an API (Active Pharmaceutical Ingredient) – Triclosan, which is used as an anti-bacterial for toothpastes and mouth wash. It manufactures speciality ingredients such as Avis (a broad spectrum UVA filter), Chlorophenesin (anti-fungal and anti-bacterial preservative), NDGA (nordihydroguaiaretic acid, an anti-oxidant and anti-ageing molecule) and Co-guar 113 and 117, speciality products used in face lotions, shampoos, liquid soaps, conditioning lotions, baby care and shaving products. Identify the company ________.
60. Who found that three quarters of mutual funds did not earn any more money than if they invested in the largest 500 companies simultaneously, using the S&P 500 stock market as bench market index and founded Vanguard as a broker-sold mutual fund company

and turned it into a no-load firm and in 1976 introduced his first index fund Vanguard 500?

61. What is common between Ferrari, Avanti an Austrian Company operating over 100 filling stations and iron horse bicycles?
62. Which company, the world's leading producer of air-compressors was started by Edward Franckel?
63. Which company is the world's largest builder of electricity grids having formed by the merger of two companies, one started by Ludwig Fredholm in 1883 and the other by Charles Eugene Lancelot Brown and Walter in 1891?
64. Lars Magnus X started his venture as a telegraph repair shop in 1876. This company X dominated the manual telephone exchange market in the early 20th Century. The world's largest ever manual telephone exchange was installed by them in Moscow. It introduced the world's first fully automatic mobile telephone system, MTA in 1956 and released one of the world's first hands-free speaker phones in the 1960s. Identify X _________.
65. Which company was started by Larry Hillblom, Adrian Dalsey and Robert Lynn?
66. Which company was originally founded by Gary Hendrix in 1982 originally focused on artificial intelligence projects and at present one of the largest makers of security software for personal computers?
67. To which company was Ratan Tata appointed as director in 1971?
68. Which company was Ratan Tata given charge in 1977, the company having to be closed in 1986?
69. Who is the designer, who designs shoes that have red lacquered soles as a permanent fixture and signature and about which shoes Jennifer Lopez has released a single from her album Love?
70. Which software company that focused on the creation of multimedia and creativity software products, was started by John Warnock and Charles Geschke?
71. Who is the only linear descendant in the House of Tata to takeover as chairman of the group?
72. What was started by Justin Berkmann as London's first club devoted to the US house music scenes?
73. What is the present-day name of the company that was started in 1895 as a cycle repair shop by Vaclav Klement and Vaclav Laurin?
74. Who owns Arab World's largest entertainment company Rotana?
75. Who is the 92-year-old audio pioneer who acquired *Newsweek* from *Washington Post* for a purchase price of $ 1 and assumption of the magazines liabilities?

76. Who founded Autodesk, the creators of the computer aided design software Auto CAD?

77. Upendra Ananth Pai, a businessman, Vaman Kudva, an engineer and T.M.A. Pai, a physician started this organization with an objective of extending financial assistance to weavers. It collected as small as 2 annas daily at the doorsteps of the depositors through its agents under its Pigmy Deposit Scheme started in 1928. It tookover the assets and liabilities of Maharashtra Apex Bank Ltd. and Southern India Apex Bank Ltd. in 1953. Its first branch was opened at Brahmavar in Dakshina Kannada district. Identify the organization ________.

78. Uday started a company in 1985 along with Sidney A. Pinto which later became the first NBFC to convert to a bank in India. Identify the bank ________.

79. He started by building a small bus line operating in the city of Sudbury in the early '50s into a large intercity bus company in Eastern Canada. In 1968 he sold these assets to Power Corporation of Canada, a diversified holding company that was previously in the hydroelectric industry. In return he received a number of shares that gave him a controlling position and allowed him to become the CEO. With the acquisition of the insurance company The Great West Life and the mutual fund company Investors Group, Power Corporation of Canada forged into financial services. Identify the personality ________.

80. This New India Assurance employee used bank receipts of public sector banks to buy stocks. He deployed well over ₹ 1,000 crore and triggered the biggest bull run in the Indian stock market. The BSE Sensex rose from around 2,000 points in January 1992 to 4,467 points in April that year. The Sensex tanked to 2,529 points in August, wiping out over ₹ 1,00,000 crore in market capitalization. Identify the personality ________.

81. Oscar Troplowitz bought Beiersdorf and was successfully producing adhesive bandages when he got information about a discovery made by Dr. Isaac Lifschutz about the emulsifying agent Eucerit, the first water in oil emulsifier able to produce a long lasting ointment base. It was used in a cosmetic cream, the world's first long lasting moisturizer. What is it?

82. Who established Metro AG, a retail and wholesale cash and carry group?

83. Which business women founded, 'Children on the Edge', a charitable organization that helps children in Eastern Europe and Asia?

84. Who is the IIM Kolkata graduate who was earlier brand manager with Procter and Gamble for Ariel and Tide and who has started village laundry service, an inexpensive, laundry chain? His Chamak outlets

wash dry and iron the laundry in 24 hours at a rate of ₹ 50 a kg. ________.

85. Which retail chain was started by Ravikumar a radio mechanic who had only studied up to 10th Standard?
86. Which company X was founded by Jeremy X along with Ashley Lloyd Jennings, who from working in a tailoring shop has created a multinational premium chain of men's haute couture and operates 77 stores in 16 countries across the globe?
87. Who was the longest serving CEO of any foreign bank in India?
88. Shyam Sunder Sharma started a company that churns out polyester staple fibres and yarns from used PET bottles. The company is the largest PET waste recycler in India with a capacity of 57,600 tonnes per annum. Name the company ________.
89. As a 16-year-old he reached Mumbai from Durgapur. His first break was as a packer, loader and a delivery boy in a tiny pouching unit. When the owners announced that they were selling the unit he came up with an offer to pay his entire earnings of ₹ 16,000 and with the promise that any profit for the first two years will go to them. Seventeen years later he bought India Foils from Metals and Mining Major Vedanta Group. His company EssDee's market capitalization is about ₹ 950 crore ________.
90. Vandana Luthra entrepreneur/mentor of VLCC has set-up a restaurant business in the name ________.
91. He is called 'Magus' (Persian for wizard) by his friends and did his Electrical Engineering from PSG College, Coimbatore. He started his career with Walchandnagar Group's Cooper Engineering. He started a company with an investment of ₹ 1,87,000 from the six founders which was involved in the manufacture of office products like copiers. Following the vacuum created by IBM quitting India his company started selling computers and came out with its own computer in 1982. He was honoured with the Honoris Causa Doctorate of Science (D.Sc.) by the IIT Kharagpur. Who is this personality?
92. Narendra Bansal was born into a family of grain merchants. He graduated from Delhi University in 1985 and was without a formal job for nearly 11 years till he set-up a firm trading in computer peripherals in 1996. He begun by selling Ethernet cards, Ethernet hubs and floppy disks. Today its portfolio straddles four verticals – mobile phones, personal computers, computer peripherals and consumer electronics. He follows four principles on which he runs his firm. They are restricting credit to 14 days, fast stock turnaround and zero obsolescence and zero bad debts. Identify the firm ________.

93. "The fragrance pays homage to Shilpa's Indian heritage and appeal to the European market", says the man who created the perfume Shilpa Shetty's S2. Who is the personality?

94. S.K. Burman started a small ayurvedic pharmacy in 1884. It grew to become a ₹ 195 crore enterprise by 1995. After several years of pondering, the Burman family renounced day-to-day management control of the company in 2001, while retaining a 69 per cent stake in it and brought in professional managers. Today it is a ₹ 3,000 crore enterprise with three strategic business units – consumer care division, consumer health division and international business division. Name the company _________.

95. Anuj Saxena, a qualified doctor, also owns a restaurant named Blue Waters and is the managing director of a certain company that produces 'Tiger Balm', which has an international heritage in its formula and is herbal in nature. His other portfolio of products includes Sensodyne, a sensitive toothpaste, AMPM mouthwash and Blistex a lip care product. Name the company.

96. Which device was built in 1978 by Nobutoshi Kihara the audio divison engineer at Sony?

97. He was influenced by his wife's death from malaria and hence saw a need for quality and effective drugs to be available on a mass scale. In 1873 he opened a store in Indianapolis. His first innovation was gelatin coating for pills and capsules. In 1890 he turned over his business to his son. His company is named after him and his company's drug production in later years include antibiotic Keflex, heart drug Dobutrex and analgesic Darvon. Who is the personality?

98. Who is acknowledged as the father of the Pentium Chip and is currently the co-founder and Managing Director of venture funds New Path Venture and NEA Indo-US ventures?

99. Devinder Pal Singh Kohli a mechanical engineer turned entrepreneur first failed in becoming an offset printing technologist. His modestly successful television manufacturing business was devastated in 1984 riots. He then served as a technical surveyor in a General Insurance Company when he reinvented himself and plunged into apparel business with the idea, 'value for money but high on fashion'. He started out as a garment manufacturer and then graduated to a speciality apparel retailer-cum-manufacturer and has around 1,400 retail outlets both company and franchisee operated. What is the brand?

100. Which nineteen-year-old heir to an Indian business empire was the founder of a youth movement called Dreaming of an Indian Awakening (DIA) in 2004, its mission, awakening young Indians to the country's rich heritage and potential?

101. Who stepped down at the age of ninety as chairman and became the chairman emeritus of a US based industry, the makers of high end audio equipment and electronic systems which he co-founded in 1953 and having brands like Infinity, Becker, Logic 7, Mark Levinson and others? The company has his name and Dinesh C. Paliwal the son of a social worker and close associate of Mahatma Gandhi is the current CEO of the company ________.

102. Ashok Mittal started in 1969 Sharda Electric Company selling off beat items such as wall brackets, tablelamps, footlights and decorative lighting pieces for interiors. He saw an opportunity in catering to burgeoning middle-class of clientele in upcoming posh South Delhi and his customers included JRD Tata. He diversified into dealing with imported marble. When ITDC put Ashok Niwas, a prime property on New Delhi's Ashoka Road, on the block he made the highest bid and for which he now has a tie-up with Ramada Plaza. The current turnover of the group is more than ₹ 2,000 crore. Identify the group ________.

103. Who was the Italian immigrant's son who got fired from Ford Motor's for what he claims in his autobiography – his ethnic roots?

104. An old man barged into Anupam Mittal's office in Mumbai and told him that he was in the matchmaking business and wanted to discuss a few things with him. He was trying to get Mittal hitched – to one of the many girls whose horoscopes were in his bag. As Mittal heard the intricacies of the trade, it occurred to him that matchmaking may be just the business his internet start-up needed to enter and started Sagaai.com which after four years became ________.

105. In 1995 at the age of 24, he caught the public imagination when his Baron International began selling 21-inch Akai Televisions for ₹ 9,999, against the average prevailing price of ₹ 15,000. The media savvy tycoon made things easier for the middle-class by exchanging old television sets for ₹ 5,000. He created two separate companies Baron International and Baron Electronics to distribute Aiwa and Akai respectively ________.

106. He joined his father's Ispat Indo in Indonesia in 1976. His first move was buying a steel plant in Trinidad and Tobago, Caribbean Ispat in 1989. He soon acquired Sircasta of Mexico, Sidbec of Canada and Ispat Hamburger Stahlwerk in Germany in 1989, 1992 and 1995 respectively. His biggest break was his 1995 acquisition of Kazakhastan's National steel plant, Karmet a heavily loss making plant employing 70,000 people and where he was not allowed to cut staff which he turned around. Identify the personality ________.

107. The son of a securities salesman, he had a knack for making money since his childhood. At age five he set-up a stand in front of his

family home and sold chewing-gum to passer-by. He sold lemonade in front of a friend's house where the traffic was heavy. In college days he would bury himself in a favourite book, one thousand ways to make $ 1,000. In 2008, he was for a period the richest man in the world and is called the oracle of Omaha. Who is he?

108. The Walchand Industries had its seed in the contracting firm (Phatak-Walchand Pvt. Ltd.) that Walchand established in partnership with a former railway clerk named.

109. Who was the owner of Bofors who owned the company from 1894 to 1896 and who played a key role in reshaping the iron manufacturer into a canon manufacturer?

110. Who is known as the 'man who broke the Bank of England'?

111. Who is the owner of the Chelsea Football Club an English Premier league football team?

112. He was born in a minor village in Jhelum district of Punjab and his father died when he was six months old. He started his hotel career as a billing clerk in Shimla's The Cecil Hotel where he helped his manager to buy The Carlton Hotel. Upon his manager's retirement he gathered all family resources to purchase The Carlton. Four years later when business was dull due to a cholera epidemic he negotiated a favourable price to takeover the management of Kolkata's Grand Hotel. After twenty-one years he was able to own his first place of employment Hotel Cecil. Identify this hotel magnate ________.

113. In which company did Pope John Paul II work during World War II to avoid deportation to Germany?

114. Whom did Harrods hire in 2007 to protect the shoe counter which had a pair of ruby, sapphire and diamond encrusted sandals launched by designer Rene Caovilla?

115. Who was the first to patent a ball point pen, whose writing implement could write on the leather he tanned?

116. She proclaimed in disgust, 'if nobody else is going to invent a dishwashing machine, I'll do it myself'. She invented the first practical dishwasher though a washing machine device was patented in 1850 by Joel Houghton. She showed her invention at the world's Colombian Exposition in Chicago. Her company later became what is known as Kitchen Aid. Identity the personality ________.

117. For which company did former US Vice-president Dick Cheney serve as the chairman and CEO from 1995 to 2000?

118. Who was the CEO of ABN-AMRO Bank's India operation who stood for the 2009 election in South Mumbai constituency?

119. Who sold the patent of the safety pin for a paltry sum of $ 400 in 1849 to W R Grace & Company to pay a man to whom he owed $ 15?
120. Identify the aviation entrepreneur who stood for the 2009 election in Bangalore constituency.
121. The Coca-Cola bottle known as hobble skirt bottle was created by _________.
122. Born Josephine Esther Mentzer she began her business selling skin care products to beauty salons and hotels. One of her favourite quotes was 'telephone, telegraph, tell a woman'. Who is she?
123. Kochouseph Chittilappilly who began his career as a supervisor in an electronics started a SSI unit in 1977 to manufacture stabilizers with ₹ 1 lakh borrowed from his father. What is that company?
124. Nainesh Nandu launched his furniture department store in Pune's Bibwewadi suburb under the name Benzer. When he found the going tough he kept some of his shops going under a new name which meant, 'beyond the Black Hole after the Milky Way' because the Benzer brand carried an 'expensive tag'. He is one of the largest furniture importers and has a big dealer network and at persent has diversified into a range of imported bathware. Identify the brand _________.
125. Who are the two entrepreneurs behind scrabulous, the online rendition of the popular board game scrabble?
126. Who was the first to patent a design of a sewing machine in 1791?
127. What was the innovative method devised by Isaac Merit Singer in partnership with Edward Clark to make people to buy his sewing machines?
128. Revlon was founded by Charles Revson in 1932? What does the 'L' in Revlon signify?
129. Which peer-to-peer (P2P) file sharing client was created by Mark Howard Gorton?
130. What was Sharuk Khan's debut business?
131. Jewish living, a bi-monthly magazine targeted at Jewish women that celebrates Jewish home, Jewish family and Jewish cultural life was launched by _________.
132. Who established the Wagh Bakri Tea Group in 1892?
133. An employee of Southland Ice Company, Joe C. Thompson, started selling milk, eggs and bread from an ice dock after he discovered that selling these convenience items was popular due to the ice's ability to preserve the items. These stores were open from 7 a.m. to 11 p.m. and is at present a chain store with more than 38,000 outlets operating around the world. Identify the name of the chain store _________.

134. Fred De Luca by borrowing $ 1,000 started his first sandwich shop when he was 17 years old, to pay for his college expenses. Promoted as Pete's Submarines it had sounded 'Pizza Marines' and hence they changed the name to "Pete's Subs". The company has more than 32,000 franchised locations in 90 plus countries. Identify the restaurant chain.

135. The scion of which hotel chain is Vikram Chatwal, the lead actor in the Vikram Singh directed, Indo French production, One Dollar Curry, where he plays a Sikh immigrant who cooks up a storm in Paris posing as a chief?

136. Ashok Patni started business by loading four gunny bags of grain in his rickety Lambretta scooter and carting them from village-to-village. He then got into marble mining with ₹ 45 lakh as seed capital. In 1998 his company entered the Guinness book of world records as the largest producer of processed marble in the world. It is also the India's first marble company to market it as a branded ware instead of a commodity. Ashok Patni himself discovered Majoli mines in Madhya Pradesh which compares with some of the finest Italian marble. Identify the company ________.

137. Suraj Mal Jalan started with a pen shop in Central Kolkata in mid-1970s and ventured into his own business as a manufacturer of writing instruments. His company has more than 50 products and at one time his brands Smart GL Line was the highest selling pen in the market. His company has association with Mitsubishi Pencil Co. Ltd., Japan, for its Uni-ball range, Bensia of Taiwan for pencils and ballpens and Lamy of Germany for premium products. Identify the company ________.

138. In 1952, Narindas Melwani left Pune to seek new fortunes in Hong Kong. He rented a shop to start tailoring in Kowloon. By 1965, they earned the reputation of 'right fit at the right price' through word-of-mouth. His shop employs digital tailoring where the customer has to only walk through these machines and measurements get recorded instantly. Though the customer profile reads a 'who's who' this establishment remains a 'one shop entity'. Identify ________.

139. Khorakiwala founded this company in the early 60s after his father Fakhruddin acquired Worli Chemical works in 1959. He set-up a biotechnology park in Aurangabad to cater to some of the world's major biopharmaceuticals. He was an early mover in the world of acquisitions and acquired Wallis laboratory in the UK in 1998. He also stabled hospitals under a corporate structure. Identify his company ________.

140. She was 34 when she tookover her father's business (with her name) after his sudden demise. She transformed barren lands to thriving cane fields to ensure committed supplies and was among the earliest to

introduce cogeneration and ethanol production in sugar industry. She was the first woman president of the Indian sugar mills association and has launched 'Contemplate', a forum that would educate ordinary people and students to appreciate art. Identify the personality _________.

141. Peto, a Jew who escaped the holocaust of World War II started making handbags at home when she married an American soldier Gerson and immigrated to United States in 1948. She started work as a handbag designer and later found her own business and her handbags are sold through exclusive boutiques which have become a status symbol. Identify the personality _________.

142. Which American blacksmith who founded one of the largest construction and agricultural equipment companies invented the first commercially successful steel plow?

143. Who resigned from being the CEO of Nokia (Nokia Mobira Oy) to start his own mobile manufacturing company Benefon Oy in 1988?

144. Born to John and Elizabeth he was brought up as a strict Baptist and became a preacher and toured the village as an evangelist. When Midland Counties Railway was extended he offered to take a group of 570 temperance campaigners from Leicester Campbell Street station to a rally in Loughborough which happened to be the first privately chartered excursion train to be advertised to the general public. He later started the 'grand circular tours' of Europe and in 1874 introduced 'circular notes' which was a precursor to the travel cheque introduced by American Bank. Identify the personality _________.

145. Why should owning home be the last step in one's life and not the first? This man kept asking himself which drove him to create Housing Development Finance Corporation Limited in 1977 and the concept of home loans was born in India. Identify this personality _________.

146. Who is the CEO of Info Watch, a company whose goal is to deal with information leakage and who is also the chairman and co-founder of Kaspersky Labs?

147. Who started as an exclusive distributor in India to market Silicon Coach Motion analysis software and later Sports Mechanics India (P) Ltd. – a sports technology company that analyses performance?

148. Who is the Swedish entrepreneur to convert a Pan Am jumbo jet and expand his hostel business by making it into spartanly furnished 65 square foot rooms with a bunk bed, an overhead luggage compartment and a flat screen television?

149. Who has launched the health and lifestyle magazine *B+VE*?

150. Pharmacologist Martin Crosby developed a female counterpart to Viagra named ________.
151. In which sport and celebrity management firm with a fairly impressive roster of clients that includes Sania Mirza, Saif Ali Khan does tennis player Mahesh Bhupathi hold a controlling stake?
152. Which Belgian born, naturalized Indian of Allahabad's Gobind Ballabh Pant Social Sciences Institute is the architect of National Rural Employment Guarantee Act?
153. Who has trademarked 'Bikram Yoga'?
154. Which Hollywood actress was married to Alfred Steele the former chairman of the Pepsi Cola Company and became a director of the company after his death in 1959?
155. Who is the chartered accountant turned businessman and member of Britains Conservative Party who started Cobra beer ten years ago to sell fine Indian lager into the European market?
156. Who launched his business career in 1969, at the age of 14 by forming a company named Lakeside Programming Group?
157. Who is the first African American to appear in a national consumer campaign in USA when Pepsi initiated a campaign targeting the Afro-American market?
158. Which timepiece manufacturer measured the micro metre (μm) for the first time and created the world's most precise measuring instrument the millionmetre, capable of measuring to thousandths of a millimetre?
159. Who built India's first cotton mill, The Bombay Spinning and Weaving Company in 1851?
160. G. Ramakrishna Reddy with his experience as a merchant banker with Mumbai based Champaklal Investment & Finance Co. set-up a securities company derived from his brothers name G. Madhusudhan Reddy. Today his company's portfolio comprises of Karaikal Port, Bijapur and Bellary Airports, Junction Mall and urban residential clusters. Identify the company ________.
161. She was named Ivy League player of the year for three consecutive seasons and was a three time All-American basketball player. Identify this personality who is at present the CEO of United Health Care the #21-ranked Fortune 500 and #1 health insurer in USA ________.
162. She started with Barcode lounge in Delhi set-up with a tie-up with EDG of Australia, then she tied-up with Merz and Krell, for writing instruments and corporate gift and followed it up with the launch of 'The O Experience' an entirely green concept of hospitality in Vasant

Vihar of New Delhi in a tie-up with UK based Exotic Nature. Identify the personality _________.

163. Who started India's first women's only rental taxi service 'For She Travel and Logistics Pvt. Ltd'?
164. Who is the first non-American to be appointed as director on the Board of Bank of America?
165. He built India's largest sugar firm by turning sick mills into shape. Seven of the eight mills owned by him in India were bought, not built. He is being called the LN Mittal of the sugar industry. Who is he?
166. Who is the cameraman behind the invention of 3D special viewing glasses?
167. We started our career as Jaspan and Jins, in the year 1938. Even our production studios opening roar is trademarked. Who are we?
168. Who is the Oscar winning costume designer of Richard Attenborough's Gandhi?
169. Who is the first African woman to head a big public company, Xerox?
170. Which corporate leader is the founder of the public-private initiative, the Health Management and Research Institute, funded by the Andhra Pradesh government?
171. Which is the iconic Italian luxury menswear that entered Indian market in 2004 with former cricketer Dilip Doshi as a partner?
172. An American investment innovator considered as a legend in the creation and marketing of mutual funds spanned his career from mutual funds management to medical research and the writing of two autobiographies. Who is this "Lion on the Wall Street"?
173. This company was founded as a wire shopping basket manufacturing company. It acquired J. Walter Thompson Company, listed on the NASDAQ and acquired Ogilvy Group in consecutive years. Presently its holdings include Grey Group, JMT, O&M, Young and Rubicam, etc. Name this British global communications services company and its founder CEO _________.
174. He began his advertising career in 1982 as an account executive at DDB. He joined J. Walter Thompson and rebranded the business as JWT by building creative reputation as the group that can do more than create solid 30-second TV commercial. He assumed the additional title of Chairman in 2005. He re-engineered JWT from a traditional ad agency into a fully integrated brand communications company. Who is this Chairman CEO?
175. Who led a group of managers from Titan's jewellery division to set-up Oyzterbay that has products similar to Titan's Tanishq?

176. She in 1982 became the first female Indian citizen to graduate from Harvard Business School and in 1994 became Morgan Stanley's first Indian recruit. She was vice-chairman of JM Morgan Stanley when she announced her move to HSBC as head of its investment banking business.
177. Who was the professional who pioneered the extensive use of PVC footwear in rural markets and was also successful with another concept-the blow moulded plastic luggage and his company Blow Plast was later acquired by Dilip Piramal Group?
178. Which is the only oil company in India that does not have a refinery of its own?
179. Which is India's first business intelligence product in the real estate space?
180. Who created Zippo, the brand best known for its pocket lighters?
181. The leading financier, who dominated the corporate finance and industrial consolidation in the Progressive era of United States, is the person responsible for the formation of General Electric and the United States Steel Corporation. Identify the financier.

Answers

1. Raman Roy
2. James F. McCann
3. Yashovardhan Saboo
4. William Sanderson
5. Sonal Agarwal
6. Welspun Retail
7. Margaret Rudkin, (The Margaret Rudkin Pepperidge Farm Cookbook)
8. Mark Zeckerberg founder, Facebook
9. Dinesh Patel
10. Wendell Rodricks
11. Amancio Ortega
12. Chris Hughes
13. Tata Chemical's wholly-owned UK arm, Brunner Monday
14. Central Bank of India
15. Tim Berners-Lee
16. Corporation Bank
17. Theodore Levitt
18. Bono

19. GE
20. Sunil Bharti Mittal
21. G. M. Rao
22. Gifford and Elizabeth Pinchot
23. R. Sriram
24. Dan and Frank
25. Sriram Srinivasan
26. Jawed Habib
27. Value Engineering
28. Sashi Chimala
29. Josiah Wedgwood.
30. Marshal Amplification
31. Lanco Group
32. Jim O'Neill
33. Madras Tyre Factory (MRF)
34. Dr. H. Elion
35. Yves Saint Laurent
36. Charak Pharma
37. Michele Taddei and Renzo Zengiaro
38. Arun Jain
39. Smiti Ruia
40. Mudra
41. Tom Peters
42. James Macgregor Burns
43. Atul Nishar
44. Tom Siebel
45. Jeff Bezos
46. Alex F. Osborn
47. Ferring Pharmaceuticals
48. John Robbins son of Irv Robbins of Baskin Robbins fame
49. Elecon (Coined from elevators and conveyors)
50. Shahnaz Husain
51. Spykar Jeans
52. Radhika Oswal
53. Kookaburra
54. Nomis

55. Jennifer Lopez
56. Vicenzo Angelino Gervasio
57. Su-Kam
58. Mysore Sandal Soap
59. Vivimed Labs Ltd.
60. John Bogle
61. Prancing horse logo (cavallino rampante)
62. Atlas Copco
63. ABB
64. Erickson
65. DHL
66. Symantec Corporation
67. The National Radio & Electronics (NELCO)
68. Empress Mills
69. Christian Louboutin
70. ADOBE Systems Incorporated
71. Sir Dorabji Tata
72. Ministry of Sound
73. Skoda Auto
74. Saudi Prince Al-Waleed bin Talal
75. Sidney Harman
76. John Walker
77. Syndicate Bank
78. Kotak Mahindra Bank
79. Paul G. Desmarais
80. Harshad Mehta
81. Nivea Cream
82. Otto Beisheim
83. Dame Anita Roddick
84. Akshay Mehra
85. Margin Free Market
86. Hackett
87. Vishwavir Ahuja former CEO of Bank of America
88. Kanpur based Ganesh Polytex Ltd.
89. Sudip Dutta
90. VLCC Alive

91. Shiv Nadar, Chairman HCL Technologies
92. Intex Technologies
93. Mark Earnshaw
94. Dabur
95. Elder Health Care Ltd. (EHCL)
96. Walkman
97. Colonel Eli Lilly and his company is Eli Lilly and Company
98. Vinod Dham
99. Koutons
100. Anand Piramal son of Ajay and Swati Piramal
101. Dr. Sydney Harman of Harman International Industries
102. Litolier Group
103. Lee Iacocca
104. Shaadi.com
105. Kabir Mulchandani
106. Lakshmi Niwas Mittal
107. Warren Edward Buffet, an American investor, industrialist and philanthropist
108. Laxmanrao Balwant Phatak
109. Alfred Noble
110. George Soros after he made a reported $ 1 billion during the 1992 Black Wednesday UK currency crisis
111. Roman Abramovich the owner of the private investment company Millhouse LLC
112. M.S. Oberoi
113. Solvay
114. Egyptian Cobra
115. John Loud
116. Josephine Cochrane
117. Halliburton
118. Meera Sanyal
119. Walter Hunt
120. Captain G.R. Gopinath
121. Earl R. Dean
122. Estee Lauder
123. V. Guard Group
124. Krome

125. Rajat and Jayant Agarwala
126. Thomas Saint a British inventor
127. Hire purchase also called time payment
128. Charles Lachman the chemist
129. Livewire
130. The Production Company 'Dreamz Unlimited'
131. Daniel Zimerman
132. Shri Narandas Desai
133. 7-Eleven
134. Subway
135. Hampshire Hotels Chain
136. R.K. Marble
137. Linc pen and plastics
138. Sam's Tailors (The word Sam made it easier for the affluent population in Hong Kong to relate with the shop and the customer profile includes George W. Bush, Bill Clinton, Prince Charles, Tony Blair, Julia Roberts, Cliff Richards, etc.)
139. Wockhardt Limited.
140. Rajashree Pathy of Rajshree Sugars
141. Judith Leiber
142. John Deere
143. Jorma Nieminen
144. Thomas Cook
145. H.T. Parekh
146. Natalya Kaspersky
147. S. Ramakrishnan
148. Oscar Dias
149. Upasna Kaamineni
150. Zestra
151. Globosport
152. Jean Dreze
153. Bikram Choudary
154. Joan Crawford
155. Karan Billimoria
156. Bill Gates
157. Ron Brown, Former US Secretary of Commerce

158. Antoine LeCoultre the founder of luxury watch manufacturer Jaeger-LeCoultre
159. Cowajee Nanabhoy Dora
160. MARG
161. Gail Boudreaux
162. Himani Modi
163. Revathi Roy
164. Mukesh Ambani
165. Narendra Murkumbi, the creator and keeper (Vice-chairman and Managing Director) of Shree Renuga Sugars.
166. G.W. 'Bilty' Bitzer
167. Tom & Jerry
168. Bhanu Athaiya
169. Ursula Burns, Chief Executive, Xerox. U.S.
170. B.Ramalinga Raju, the tainted founder of Sathyam Computer Services.
171. Canali
172. Jack Dreyfus
173. Sir Martin Sorrell's WPP plc (Wire and Plastic Products plc)
174. Bob Jeffery
175. Vasant Nangia
176. Naina Lal Kidwai
177. Jal Engineer
178. IBP formerly Indo-Burma Petroleum
179. P. E. Analytics, founded by Samir Jasuja, CEO
180. George G. Blaisdell
181. John Pierpont Morgan (J.P. Morgan)

7 ADVERTISEMENT

Questions

1. For which brand was John Cameron Swayze a spokesperson for live torture tests on television commercials that had as tagline, 'Takes a Licking and Keeps on Ticking'?
2. For which product was the 1970s campaign 'This Buds for you' created by D'Arcy Masius Benton & Bowles?
3. What was introduced by Alexander Walker in terms of labelling in Johnnie Walker bottles?
4. The song Mehbooba from *Sholay* was used to market ________.
5. With which company did Pepsico file a case for using its energy drink Gatorade's tagline 'rehydrate, replenish, refuel'?
6. Who is the first male to be featured in a Lux commercial?
7. Which company owns the Jack Daniel's brand of spirits?
8. Which brand has come up with a 'Good bye 1984' that takes a dig at Apple, its ipad and its 1984 advertisement to launch the Macintosh?
9. For which product was India's first ever 3D advertisement campaign created?
10. Which company ran commercial advertisements that included a dramatization showing Frank the co-founder of Pizza Hut coming to a Pizza Hut stockholders' meeting wearing a competitors apron, saying, "Sorry, guys. I found a better pizza."?
11. Gabbar Singh was the first villain to endorse a product and endorsed ________.
12. Which products advertisement has lizards impersonating frogs and a team of Clydesdale horse?
13. Which company entered through a venture with DCM Group in 1995, found that AIDS awareness theme was most relevant in India and hence for its advertisement chose the image of a collage of coloured

condoms and a montage of picture of people's faces rearranged to spell AIDS?

14. What was the name of the campaign of International Advertising Association, seeking world leaders to take the right decision during the Copenhagen summit for climate change?
15. Which company in its print advertisement says that Mars bound Rover's gearbox, Solar panel drives and actuators rotating the cameras ran on their precision ball bearings?
16. Who was the first brand ambassador of Mysore Sandal Soap?
17. He spent two years in the army during World War II and then joined Grey agency where he quickly became creative head. Four years later, with Ned Doyle and Max Dane, he started his own agency. He always used to carry a card with a self-admonition message, 'May be he's right'. He is best remembered for his campaigns for Volkswagen and Avis. Identify the personality _________.
18. Whose television advertisement has the signature line, 'Protect what's good'?
19. Which company ran a controversial advertising which it was forced to withdraw where it claimed that the toilet seat was cleaner than kitchen work surfaces?
20. Which company's advertisement campaign introduces Titus Moody a baker complete with horse and wagon which happen to be one of the longest running campaigns in television history?
21. Name the brand for which Alisha Chinai made her debut as an advertisement jingle singer?
22. This company encouraged people to duck their responsibilities on December 7, 2003 and asked them to take a half-day-off and enjoy their product at the participating bars. One can enter a contest, wherein he had to enter the names of three friends and stood a chance of winning $ 25 coupons. Those three friends in turn, got similar messages to win their $ 25 coupons. This campaign increased the brand awareness of the product from 38 per cent to 57 per cent. Identify the product _________.
23. Which company's commercial was criticized by feminists on the ground that it insinuated laundry as a feminine job for the words, 'Your mother, your grandmother, her mother, they all did the laundry, may be even a man or two'?
24. What is common between Victor Kiam, Dave Thomas, Lee Iacocca and William Schreyer?
25. Which company shortly after the September 11, 2001 attack gave an American flag as a full page colour advertisement in *New York Times*

and *Washington Post* which said, 'Remove from newspaper, place in window, embrace freedom', with its signature in small characters on the lower left?

26. For which Bajaj product advertisement which was set up at Heng Deng in Shenghai did Jackie Chan portray a monk?
27. Whose advertisement features the rendition by children's choir of Peter Allen's, 'I still call Australia Home', set to a footage of Australian scenery?
28. Which automobile manufacturer organized, 'Securing borders drive' which involved NCC cadets traversing on an eighteen day drive from Wagah border through Rann of Kutch and Longewala battle field in Jaisalmer to promote relations between India and its neighbouring countries?
29. Which soap manufacturing company in India owns a proprietary geographical identification tag on the soap it manufactures?
30. He landed a job as a reporter on the *Peoria* journal. Later he joined the advertising department of Cadillac. He later joined *Erwin Wasey* as copy chief, and in 1935 set up his own agency. By the time he died his agency was one of the biggest in the world outside New York. He is best remembered for his campaign for Marlbaro cigarettes. Identify the personality ________.
31. For which motor car did Oglivy feature the famous title, 'the loudest noise comes from an electric clock' which was followed by 607 words of factual information?
32. Which ice cream company is behind 'Free Cone Day' an annual event held between late March and early May in which more than one million free cones are given away each year, prompting the company's ad slogan 'Be One In A Million'?
33. Which company is known for its free flight promotion where it offered in 1992 a free ticket to all those who bought its products for more than £ 100 but was overwhelmed when huge numbers of customers started buying its products not because they wanted the actual appliances, but simply because they wanted the tickets, which eventually led to its sale to Candy?
34. Which shaving equipment major is part of the 'Women Against Lazy Stubble' (W.A.L.S.), a group of young women looking to attract all like-minded women across India, who believe that men should make efforts to keep themselves groomed?
35. For which advertisement campaign did John Moschitta Jr., a contestant of the ABC show 'that's incredible' who could speak more than 500 words in 54 seconds as a motor mouth, who speed talked his way through lunch, hired an employer conducted a board meeting

and consummated a business deal on the phone all in less than a minute?

36. For which product was the 'Machar Mukti Abhiyan' (Freedom from mosquitoes) campaign launched?
37. Which auto major, advertised in its print advertisement that Marilyn Monroe, John F. Kennedy and Bruce Springsteen owned their products?
38. What does the wing-foot symbol of the company Goodyear signify?
39. What is the relationship between Mitsubishi and its Logo?
40. Which company in 1952 advertised its shirts as "the status symbol of competent sportsman"?
41. Which cricketer was the star of Siyaram J. Hampstead clothing when his name cropped up in a betting scandal?
42. Toyota has advertised that its vehicles have been refined by using the concept of Genchi Genbutsu. What does it mean?
43. Which product is known for its commercial featuring Annie Little sporting the song, 'Fly me away' with the slogan 'Book in 60 seconds'?
44. The campaign for 'Real Beauty' which features real woman not models focusing on promoting real natural beauty, articulated through their slogan 'real women have curves' was launched in 2004 by ________.
45. Which telecom major has tied dinghy boats to hoardings in major cities at points that are prone to water logging which can be lowered by their company volunteers and be used to ferry stranded passengers when the cities get inundated with rain water?
46. Against which brand of Gufic Biosciences which focus on herbal health care products has the American cosmetic major Estee Lauder launched a trademark infringement case that the said brand is deceptive to its 'Clinique brand'?
47. For which product did Vijay Amritraj endorse the brand and when his popularity started to fade Gavaskar was brought in 1975. By 1981, Gavaskar had become extremely popular and was endorsing many products and fearing that the consumer will get confused Kapil Dev was chosen to endorse the product. What is the product?
48. Which Indian advertising campaign was carried out first in twenty-two editions of the *Financial Times* on 10 December, 2004?
49. Which company used the advertisement 'Nickel, Nickel', the first advertising jingle ever broadcast throughout the United States which was translated into fifty-five languages?
50. Which is the second company from Kolkata to have Sharukh Khan as an ambassador after Emami?
51. Who was the first cricketer to star in a commercial?

52. Which airline used for its advertising the musical theme 'The Flower Duet' by Leo Delibes along with the 'Face' advertisement?
53. The only product for which bollywood actress Rekha featured in a commercial is ________.
54. Who was the first baby to appear on a Johnson & Johnson baby powder label?
55. In December 2005, Honda released the 'The Impossible Dream' a two-minute panoramic advertisement filmed in New Zealand, Japan and Argentina. Whose 1960 musical song was it from?
56. Which was the Broadway musical inspired by the fictional Arrow collar man?
57. Which brands creative platform seeks to reawaken bottled up instincts and to encourage who and what we are fundamentally with the signature line 'We are Animals'?
58. Which product was advertised by sticking a yellow Ford Cortina to a billboard with the tagline 'it also sticks handles to teapots'?
59. Who has lent his voice to the animated parrots that have replaced Zoozoo in Vodafone advertisement?
60. Who has introduced a skin lightening application for Facebook in India enabling users to make their skin whiter in their profile pictures?
61. Which two companies produced the family movies, *'Secrets of the Mountain'* and *'The Jenson Project'*, which featured characters using their brands?
62. Which company has chosen Luba Fishman a great grandmother about to celebrate her hundredth birthday as the poster woman for its real beauty campaign with the slogan 'does true beauty have an age limit'? Is designed to avoid 'beauty stereotypes?
63. For which product did the model (Shimona) dance on sports pitch to get the campaign of the century award in Indian advertising?
64. The sheet music of the commercial using the song, 'I'd like to buy the world', is an all time favourite and continues to sell even today. Which company did it?
65. Alyque Padamsee, the advertising guru remarked, "it's like throwing the baby with the bathtub, and having Krishna without a flute". Which advertising was he referring to?
66. After becoming a huge internationally recognized brand Shahnaz Husain Herbals became a case study at Harvard Business School due to a factor related to advertising. What is that reason?
67. Which company has tied-up with music maestro A.R. Rahman for using his Oscar winning Jai Ho track for its television commercial?

68. Who made her debut as a singer through an advertisement Jingle for Farex?
69. Rupert Fernandes wrote the original tune "You and I" which was used by __________ in its famous ad campaigns over the years.
70. The first Asian Advertising Festival planned as an Asian equivalent to Cannes Adfest is _________.
71. The only Indian actress who endorsed for both the brands Coke and Pepsi in India was _________.
72. Which automobile X used the Dr. X theme for its marketing campaign that included Dr. X a tall lean professor with a white lab coat and his assistants Elephant Engine Ernie, Shifty Sidney, Wind Tunnel Waldo and Hy Spy?
73. For which company did BBDO create the animated parrot Sharpie, to deliver its message in the form of a jingle that went as 'Look sharp, Feel sharp, be sharp…..'?
74. For promoting which product was an interactive campaign employed by having magician Ugesh Sarcar to perform his tricks involving the product in crowded areas in front of unsuspecting spectators which was followed by free distribution of the product and snapshots of which were aired as television commercials?
75. Which company launched its integrated global marketing campaign coded 'Everybody On' during the 53rd Annual GRAMMY Awards in February 2011 and started with a one minute television spot that featured their products and displayed how technology enables people to connect with their passions?
76. Who introduced pixel advertising by creating a website called 'The Million Dollar Homepage' that allowed advertisers to buy advertisement space measured in pixels on the homepage?
77. Which campaign won the Grand Effie award for the Best Integrated Campaign of the Year 2009?
78. Which company made changes to the original St. Nick and created the character in a red and white costume as Santa Claus to promote their product?
79. Which is the first Indian Commercial to win at Canes?
80. Which company created the first-ever testimonial ad for Pond's Cold Cream in 1925?
81. This company has made advertisements that are interesting like the politician who is glued to his chair, the hen that laid unbreakable eggs, the overflowing bus and the joint family that reduces to fall apart. The successful campaigns were created by Oglivy and Mather. Identify the company _________.

82. For which product did Pooja Bedi and Mark Robinson create erotic history on desi television telling Indians for the first time that sex was fun?

83. This Indian pen maker has undertaken an environment-friendly initiative, 'Refill More', through a media campaign which emphasizes that since refills contain lower quantity of plastic it encourages them to reuse ballpens with new refills instead of replacing the pen. The company has planned drop boxes in 750 schools in metro cities where students can drop-off empty refills and pens. Identify the company ________.

84. Which company has introduced for its campaign where for the first time You Tube Videos have been made round in design and is part of its existing 'Ready to Roll' campaign?

85. Which washing machine company in 2000 carried an advertisement from the 'Wash Counsellors', which offered to mail consumers a booklet on 'How to Buy the Right Washing Machine' which was a step-by-step process to promote their washing machines as also this direct marketing enabled them to create a database of potential consumers?

86. Which oblate spheroid product of Perfetti Van Melle Corporation's Indian advertisement translates as, 'Eat 'the product' and ignite the fire in your mind and is based on the situation where the loser eats the product and becomes a winner?

87. For the advertisement of which brand was the image of the naked red haired, hands behind her head and wind in her hair, Ruby, the size 16 doll was created?

88. The products advertisements have been stepping stones for leading models such as Arjun Rampal, Sushma Reddy, Aryan Vaid, Rahul Dev and Mallika Sherawat into Bollywood and credited with making the finest cardigans and pullovers from Merino wool.

89. An advertisement released in 1998 flaunted models Milind Soman and Madhu Sapre clad in nothing but a python and a shoe. This sparked-off angry protest and the advertisements were withdrawn. What is the product?

90. Whose advertisement had a signature tune from Mozart's fifth symphony, and its jingles were one of the earliest tune compositions of A.R. Rahman?

91. Which clothing company's advertisement done by photographer Oliviero Toscani were unrelated to clothes sold by the company and included scenes of a person dying with AIDS, panicking crowds jumping-off of a sinking ship and an unwashed new born baby, the only caption in the pictures being the company Logo?

92. Which was the first perfume advertisement to feature a woman wearing pants?
93. Which company launched an advertisement highlighting the durability of its product by unleashing a Gorilla on its product?
94. Which company secured a new Guinness world record for the fastest painted billboard completion for which a stunt was conceived to illustrate and emphasize the fast acting formulation of the product?
95. Name the coffee chain that CNN has got tied-up for an interactive promotion ________.

Answers

1. Timex
2. Budweiser
3. Slanted label where each label is slanted at 24 degrees
4. Strepsils
5. Heinz (The Heinz advertisement for 'Glucon-D Isotonik uses 'rehydrates fluids, replenishes vital salts and recharges glucose', a sounding tagline)
6. Marlon Brando
7. Brown-Forman
8. Motorola Xcom
9. Audi
10. Papa John
11. Britannia Glucose D Biscuits
12. Budweiser
13. Benetton
14. Hopenhagen
15. Timken
16. Mahendra Singh Dhoni
17. Bill Bernbach
18. Tetra-Pak
19. Dettol
20. Pepperidge Farm
21. Farex
22. Smirnoff
23. Clorox
24. They are senior company executives who appeared in testimonial ads

25. Kmart
26. Bajaj Discover
27. Qantas
28. FIAT India for its Fiat Grande Punto 90 HP Multijet
29. Karnataka Soaps and Detergents Limited, the manufacturers of Mysore Sandal Soap
30. Leo Burnett
31. Rolls Royce
32. Ben & Jerrys
33. Hoover
34. Gillette
35. FedEx
36. Dabur's Odomos
37. Chevrolet
38. Mercury, the God of Trade and Commerce and more than that a swift messenger for all God's of mythology
39. Mitsu means three and hishu refer to water chestnut and hence rhombus.
40. Lacoste
41. South African Cricketer Hansie Cronje
42. The philosophy of 'go and see'
43. Kindle
44. Dove
45. Aircel
46. 'Skincliniq Stretch Nil' (Clinique is one of the top leading global brands of Estee Lauder and has been in international markets since 1968.
47. Palmolive shaving cream
48. India Shining
49. Pepsi
50. Linc pens
51. Farokh Engineer for Brylcreem. (He was perfect competition for Dennis Compton – the original Brylcreem boy)
52. British Airways
53. Lakme beauty lotion
54. The company's first president Robert Wood Johnson's grand daughter Mary Lea Johnson Richards

55. Man of La Muncha sung by Andy Williams
56. Helen of troy in 1923
57. Wrangler
58. Araldite
59. Boman Irani
60. Vaseline
61. Wal-Mart and Procter & Gamble
62. Dove
63. Cardbury Dairy Milk
64. Coca-Cola
65. Liril's new advertisement without its famous water fall scene
66. No advertising
67. Kolkata-based Century Plywoods
68. Alisha Chinai
69. Hutch
70. SPIKES Asia
71. Aishwarya Rai
72. Oldsmobile
73. Gillette
74. Full Toss from Parle
75. Hewlett-Packard
76. Alex Tew
77. The Times of India's (TOI) 'Teach India Let's Learn to Teach' (Teach India) campaign on December 16, 2009.
78. Coca-Cola – advertisement done by a Swedish firm Haddon Sundblom
79. Ericsson cellphone *"One Black Coffee"* by Prasoon Pandey, Corcoise Films
80. J. Walter Thompson (JWT)
81. Fevicol
82. The Kamasutra campaign of 1993
83. Linc Pens and Plastics Ltd.
84. Cadbury's to promote its Rollpack
85. Swedish white goods giant
86. Mentos
87. The Body Shop
88. Monte Carlo

89. Tuff shoes
90. Titan
91. The United Colours of Benetton Advertisement for Benetton range of clothing
92. Charlie model Shelley Hack
93. The advertisement ran for 15 years – American Tourister
94. Saridon
95. Barista Coffee Chain

Questions

1. Who acquired Universal Studios from Panasonic in 1995?
2. Which ceramics giant acquired Yashica Company Ltd., in October 1983?
3. Which company has acquired Yardley in certain markets including Asia, Middle East and Australia?
4. MTR Foods was acquired in 2007 by ________.
5. Who acquired 52 per cent of MphasiS in 2004?
6. Who acquired Kanbay, a player in the financial, life-sciences and consumer and industrial product spaces in the year 2004?
7. Which Indian company acquired vredestein, a blue-chip, hi-end Dutch tyre manufacturer in 2009 and Dunlop, South Africa in 2006?
8. Who acquired Blue Dart, for ₹ 700 crore in 2004 and became the first international express and Logistics Company to offer domestic and international services of its own in India?
9. Which company acquired the entire domestic formulation business of Piramal Health Care for about ₹ 17,000 crore?
10. Who acquired Cimmco Spinners (26,208 spindles) from SK Birla in 2003, Spentx Industries (29,232 spindles) from RPG Group, Ahmedabad unit from Tai Group, Indo Rama Textiles and Tashkent To'ytepa Tekstils (2,20,000 spindles) from Uzbekistan government in 2006?
11. This company's flagship banking product was flexcube and this company was acquired by Oracle Corporation. Name the company.
12. Who founded a company IIS Infotech which was acquired by Xansa and also co-founded Indian Angel Network and industry apex body Nasscom?

13. Which Indian company acquired Ecu line – a Belgium based Logistics Company which happens to be the first global acquisition by an Indian logistics company?
14. Which Indian company acquired a seventy per cent stake in two Middle East companies Strategic Food International, Dubai and Al Sallan Food Industries in Oman both regional players in biscuit and cookies in the GCC markets with brands like Nutro, Family Choice and Baker's Pride?
15. Which Indian company in 2007 acquired the Frankfurt SLI Sylvania, a Dutch lighting major for $ 300 million which helped it add a portfolio of brands like Sylvania, Concord, Marlin, Lumiance, Claude, Linolite, etc.?
16. Which airline acquired Morris Air and Muse Air?
17. Who owns the ACK media that acquired Amar Chitra Katha, Tinkle and Karadi Tales from India Book House?
18. Who acquired Singapore based Derma Rx a chain of skin care clinics based in South East Asia founded by Dr. S.K. Tan and Janifer Yeo?
19. This company started-off with a small oral formulation unit in Daman in the late 1990s when it bagged a manufacturing contract from Cipla. It recently acquired TVC Life Science and had also merged with Vaibhav Health Care its sister concern. Name the company.
20. Who was the original producer of Old Spice, from whom the company was acquired by Procter and Gamble?
21. Who acquired Desiya a Gurgaon based business-to-business service provider in hospitality industry founded by Amit Taneja?
22. Who acquired the three tea companies – Bareilly Tea Holdings, Doom Dooma Tea Company and the Moran Tea Company, India between 2005 and 2007?
23. Who acquired Calvin Klein Inc. in December 2002?
24. Which start-up the maker of Sidekick smartphone was acquired by Microsoft in 2008?
25. Who in 1933 acquired the *Washington Post* in a bankruptcy auction?
26. Which company acquired Nutrine, India's largest confectionery maker from the Andhra Pradesh based B.V. Reddy family with a single cheque of ₹ 250 crore?
27. Which company was created by the merger of Yawata Iron & Steel and Fuji Iron & Steel?
28. Which Indian company is acquiring the Turkish personal care products company Hobi Kozemtik Group, a market leader in the hair gel category?

29. Which Pharma Company was created by the merger of Ciba Geigy and Sandoz both Swiss Companies with long histories?
30. Which company acquired the personal computes hardware division of IBM, the company that revolutionized the personal computer business across the globe?
31. This pharmaceutical company acquired Warren Pharmaceuticals Ltd. and Warren Laboratories Pvt. Ltd., in 1999. It also acquired Karvol a brand of Solvay Pharma India Limited, a subsidiary of Solvay Multinational Group. It has created brands like Glychek (anti-diabetic, MCBM 69 (nerve nourisher) and Atherochek (statin and vitamin combination for cardiac patients). Identify the company _________.
32. Which group founded in 1966 and at present part of the French Luxury Group, PPR entered India in 2007 with the Murjanis but signed on with Genesis Colours in 2010?
33. Which luxury brand was founded in 1934 by brothers Giovanni and Giacomo that entered India in 2004 and has a partnership with Genesis Colours to run the brand name in India?
34. JK Ansell Ltd. the manufacturers and sellers of Kamasutra condoms is a 50-50 joint venture between JK Ansell and _________.
35. Which Indian company acquired the Namaste Group, a US based hair care company catering to the needs of consumers of African descent and Turkey based Hobi Kozmetik a skin care products company?
36. Who has entered into a ₹ 100 crore 50:50 joint venture with a corporate entity, Better Value Brands to launch a global chain of restaurants called 'Indii'?
37. IOT Infrastructure and Energy Services Ltd., is a 12-year-old company whose portfolio of completed projects include 3 million Kilolitres of petroleum product storage, 243 km. of cross-country petroleum product pipelines, utilities and offsites for refineries, aviation fuel handling systems, LPG storage and bottling facilities and is a joint venture between Indian Oil and _________.
38. Which company acquired a majority control of CRISIL in 2005?
39. International Container Trans-shipment Terminal at Vallarpadam, India's first container trans-shipment hub, is a BOT project between Cochin Port Trust and _________.
40. With which Indian company did Sweden's Volvo Bus Corp enter India as a joint venture, whose stake it has recently bought out?
41. To whom was DuPont's subsidiary Invista, the world's largest integrated fibre, resin and intermediates company sold in 2003?
42. Which company was acquired by Reckitt Benckiser in 2010 that added Durex and Scholl to its portfolio?

43. Which company, the world's second largest cement maker, established its presence in India by acquiring ACC in 2005 and Gujarat Ambuja Cements in early 2006?
44. Which company was formed in 2001 by the merger of two large New Zealand dairy cooperatives and the New Zealand dairy board?
45. Who established Metro AG, a retail and wholesale cash and carry group?
46. Who acquired Gillette stationary product's business, Papermate, Parker and Waterman in the year 2000?
47. Which company has acquired the hydrogenated vegetable oil brand Dalda from Hindustan UniLever Ltd.?
48. Which company Acquired Guinness World Records from HIT Entertainments in 2008?
49. With which company did Tetra–Pak form a 20:80 joint venture when it entered India in 1987?
50. Which company along with Chennai based philanthropic organization SMILE (Selfless Movement Improving Life Everywhere) executed a campaign in 2003 to inspect and rectify cistern defects in 5,000 toilets/bathrooms at Thirumala, which gets an average of 40,000-50,000 pilgrims per day and over 1,00,000 visitors on festival days saving 1,50, 000 litres of water?
51. Which Indian company in 2005 acquired Williamson Tea which had 18 tea gardens spread across the Brahmaputra valley in Assam and an annual production of 20 million kg. from the UK based Magor family?
52. Which Indian company acquired the German wind power company RE power, the only producer of 5MW wind power turbine in the world?
53. Which Indian company has a tie-up with French fragrance major Coty to bring down the Adidas range of personal care products such as deo spray, body spray, shower gel, after shave and eau de toilette?
54. 'Best Price Modern Wholesale' is a 50:50 joint venture between _________.
55. Energetic Lighting India Pvt. Ltd., a producer of CFL lamps with manufacturing facilities at Manessar and Bawal is a 50:50 joint venture between US based Energetic Lighting Inc. and _________.
56. Which company has entered into a lease agreement with the state owned Assam Tea Corporation to manage two of its estates – Longai and Ishabheel – which collectively produce 6,00,000 kg. of black tea annually?
57. Which company bought Joseph Nathan, Allen & Hanbury's and Meyer Laboratories in 1947, 1958 and 1978 respectively?

58. Which Indian company has agreed to buy coal reserves of Australian firm Linc Energy for a $ 500 million ($ 455 million) which involves purchasing the Australian company's 100 per cent interest in the Galilee Coal tenement in the Galilee Basin, Queensland?
59. Who started Krishna Maruti a joint venture to supply car seats to Maruti and the company has now expanded to add mirrors, head rests, seat trims, door trims, seat liners, carpets and fuel tanks?
60. Which company broke-off franchise partnership with Planet retail in March '08 and formed a 51:49 JV with Reliance retail since April '08 and whose product was positioned as an aspirational brand from 2001 to early 2008 and now repositioned as an affordable brand?
61. Which group acquired Formica Corporation in 2007?
62. Who acquired Pixar in 1986, which was started as the graphics groups part of the Computer Division of Lucas Film?
63. Philips Morris launched this product via a joint venture in 1983 when it bombed. It again relaunched the product in 2001 manufacturing the product, a granulated quick mix powdered drink, near Hyderabad. What is the product?
64. Which Indian company acquired vredestein, a blue-chip, hi-end Dutch tyre manufacturer in 2009 and Dunlop, South Africa in 2006?
65. Which is the first joint stock publishing company of Republic of India incorporated by __________.
66. Which raw materials company did Nirma purchase in November 2007 making it among the top ten Soda Ash manufacturers in the world?
67. What is the brand that has been created by a 50:50 partnership between Hidesign and Kishore Biyani of Future Group?
68. Who purchased the Radisson Hotels in 1962 and is still owned by his company?
69. Which company acquired a 45 per cent stake in London branch of Lazard Brothers in 1919 and also acquired *Financial Times, Longman* and the educational division of Simon & Schuster?
70. Which cement company did Lafarge acquire in 2001 to become the then largest manufacturer of cement in the world?
71. Which company was created by the merger of Yawata Iron & Steel and Fuji Iron & Steel?
72. Which brewing giant was formed in August 2004 when Belgium's Interbrew bought Brazilian brewer Ambev?
73. Which company has joined with American industrial product major Eagle Pischer to manufacture and market automobile and Valve

Regulated Lead Acid (VRLA) batteries in India under the brand Luminous-Eagle Pischer?

74. Which group acquired Bangalore based mobile retail chain MobileNXT Teleservices and relaunched it as 'Hoop' and extended it to retailing jewellery brands like Lucera, Revv, Miki, Pearls, Golden Dreams and Hoop?
75. Which company has acquired the US Company Natrol and post-acquisition has received Good Manufacturing Practices (GMP) certification from US Natural Products Association and has launched 'Immune Boost' which enhances the body's natural immune mechanism?
76. To whom did Wal-Mart sell its 16 outlets in South Korea which have been rebranded as E-Mart stores?
77. The Rio Tinto Group is primarily focused on extraction of minerals and is among the world leaders in aluminium, iron ore, copper, uranium, coal and diamonds. Where does it get its name from?
78. Which company acquired the mobile device's division of Siemens AG?
79. Which Indian companies have secured the rights for the El Mutun mines in Bolivia, which is one of the largest reserves of iron ore in the world, with reserves of 40 billion ton tons?
80. Which engineering to education conglomerate had a joint venture with Kerala Vaidyasala and which it has now completely bought out from Kurup family?
81. Which Indian company has acquired Griffin coal mines in Western Australia?
82. Who has proposed to buy RC2 Corporation in North America the toymaker who makes Thomas the Tank Engine products after declining birth-rate eroded its demand at home?
83. Which Indian company has taken a majority stake in a joint venture with China's third largest tractor company, Yancheng tractor owned by the Yueda Group?
84. The very first business started by Sir Richard Branson, the British and Irish music retail chain Virgin Megastores has now been renamed as __________.
85. Who is the first Indian to form a foreign collaboration when in 1833 he teamed up with Carr Gordon and Princep?
86. Which company sold its 49 per cent stake in Citroen back to Michelin in 1973 thereby withdrawing from PARDEVI agreement (participation in Development Industries) when Citroen's financials became weak due to oil crisis?

87. Name the joint venture of Bharti Airtel and Indian Farmers Fertiliser Cooperative _________.
88. Which Indian Pharmaceutical company entered into a strategic alliance with Japan's Kyowa Pharmaceuticals to market finished formulations in Japan?
89. This company spins out from Pepsi Co. in 1997 and licenced KFC, Pizza Hut, Taco Bell brands worldwide. In 2002 it underwent a merger with Yokeshire and renamed as Yum Brands. Name the company _________.
90. Which company owns the American food conglomerate Quaker Oats?
91. The health food drink brand 'Viva' and 'Maltova' was acquired by the multinational SmithKline Beecham Consumer Health Care (SBCH) for ₹ 86.25 crore from which company?
92. Pioneer Embroideries Limited acquired 'Hakoba' brand and embroidery manufacturing facilities from _________.
93. Name the joint venture between HLL life care and Acumen Fund that emerged as a network of 20-25 bedded no frills maternity hospitals catering to lower-income group category.
94. The acquisition of which company in 2006 led Whirlpool Corporation to be the largest home appliance maker in the world?

Answers

1. Seagrams
2. Kyocera
3. WIPRO Consumer Care
4. Orkla Foods
5. Texas based Electronic Data System
6. Capgemini
7. Apollo Tyres
8. DHL, the Deutsche Post World Net Owned Logistics Company
9. Abbott Ltd.
10. Mukund Choudhary
11. I-flex
12. Saurabh Srivastava
13. All Cargo Global Logistics
14. Britannia
15. Havells

16. South West Airlines
17. Samir Patil and Shripal Morakhia
18. Kaya the wholly-owned subsidiary of Marico
19. Ankur Drugs and Pharmaceuticals
20. The Shulton Company founded in 1934 by William Lightfoot Schultz
21. Travelguru.com founded by Ashwin Damera
22. Mcleod Russel who also own Eveready which deals with FMCG goods such as batteries, flash lights and packet tea – the bulk tea is under Mcleod Russel banner
23. The shirt maker Philips Van Heusen
24. Danger
25. Eugene Meyer
26. Godrej
27. Nippon Steel
28. Dabur India
29. Novartis
30. Lenova
31. Indoco Remedies
32. Bottega Veneta
33. Canali
34. Raymond
35. Dabur
36. Sanjeev Kapoor, celebrated chef, TV show host, cookbook author, restaurateur and food consultant
37. Oiltanking of Germany
38. Standard & Poor's (S&P) Ratings Group
39. DP World
40. Azad Group's Jaico Automobile Engineering Co. Pvt. Ltd.
41. Koch Industries
42. SSL International Plc.
43. Holcim
44. Fonterra
45. Otto Beisheim
46. Newell Rubbermaid
47. Bungee
48. Jim Pattison Group
49. National Dairy Development Board

50. Parryware
51. Mcleod Russel
52. Suzlon
53. Cavinkare
54. Bharti Enterprises and US based Wal-Mart
55. Delhi based V.P. Electromech
56. Jay Shree Tea
57. Glaxo Laboratories
58. Adani Enterprises
59. Ashok Kapur
60. Marks and Spencer
61. Fletcher Building Group
62. Steve Jobs
63. Tang
64. Apollo Tyres
65. Kandathil Varghese Mappillai
66. Searles Valley Minerals Inc.
67. Holii
68. Curt Carlson
69. Pearson PLC
70. Blue Circle Industries
71. Nippon Steel Corporation
72. Inbev
73. SAR Silicon
74. Gitanjali Group
75. Plethico Pharmaceuticals
76. Shinsegae, a local retailer
77. It comes from Rio Tinto River which flows red due to acid mine drainage
78. BenQ Corporation
79. Jindal Steel & Power Ltd.
80. Yash Birla Group
81. Lanco Infratech
82. Tomy Co.
83. Mahindra and Mahindra
84. Zavvi Entertainment Group

85. Dwaraka Nath Tagore
86. FIAT
87. IFFCO Kisan Sanchar
88. Lupin Pharmaceutical Ltd., Mumbai
89. Tricon Global Restaurants Inc.
90. Pepsi Co. since 2001
91. Jagatjit Industries
92. M/s. Fancy Corporation Limited at Borivali, Mumbai
93. Life Spring Hospitals
94. Maytag Corporation

Questions

1. The inaugural flight by Airbus A 380 was from Singapore to ________.
2. Which is the country to become the first right hand drive market to have the SLS AMG, the aviation inspired sports car with gull wing designed doors?
3. Which uniform was first introduced by Malaysia-Singapore Airline which was worn by flight stewardesses and later became a prominent symbol of the corporate image of Singapore Airlines?
4. Who are the Brettonwood sisters?
5. Who developed the short messaging service (SMS) in 1984?
6. Which company invented the laser printer and mouse?
7. Which is the world's longest continuously heated and insulated pipe-line?
8. Where is the first Indian clinic, of United Kingdom based Bourn Hall Clinic, founded by Roberts Edwards, the 2010 medicine Nobel prize winner proposed to be located?
9. Why is a hammer kept on display at Haier's headquarters?
10. The significance of June 20, 1910 is that it marks the establishment of ________.
11. Which is at present proposed biggest mall in India?
12. Godrej has chalked out what it calls a '3 by 3' strategy for its international foray! What is it?
13. Which company is the world's largest producer of tea?
14. Which company has launched an initiative 'Samrudhi', which aims to educate farmers in the latest farming technologies and practices?
15. Which is the largest manufacturer of sunglasses globally?
16. Who was donated the first car to be produced by Maruti?

17. Whose public issue, the first public issue by any microfinance in Asia, received massive response from investors with the issue getting over subscribed a 13.64 times?
18. Which is the world's largest non-profit organization and set up in the US nearly 120 years ago?
19. Which is India's first million square foot mall?
20. In 1973, Yashica commenced a project it coded 'Top Secret Project 130'. What was it?
21. Which is the only private player to have a container freight station at Kolkata port, the other two players being the government-owned Balmer Lawrie and Central Ware Housing Corporation each with capacities of 3,000 containers a month?
22. Which is the first figure to represent a commercial undertaking at Madame Tussaud's wax museum in London in 1994?
23. Who along with agricultural insurance company has formulated an insurance scheme for coconut trees on a pilot basis along with the support of state governments?
24. Colgate is publicly listed in only two countries. What are the countries?
25. Which camera did John Glenn take to space in 1962 aboard Freedom 7?
26. Who made the world's first all electric compact calculator on relay technology in 1957?
27. Which company brought out the first standards-compliant keyboard that bears Indian National Rupee (INR) symbol?
28. Leonard Marraffino invented in 1955 a method to get stripes in tooth-paste and sold his patent to UniLever. Under what name was the first striped toothpaste launched in 1960?
29. Which is the first hotel in Indian hospitality industry to offer garden rooms – where rooms have their own private garden?
30. Which is the world's largest and India's first LEED (Leadership in Energy and Environment Design) Platinum rated hotel?
31. What is MoMo (Mobile Monday)?
32. Which is the first Indian dotcom to list on a US stock exchange?
33. What was the millionaire scheme introduced by Sistema Shyam Teleservices brand MTS (formerly known as Rainbow)?
34. This company's flagship banking product was flexcube and this company was acquired by Oracle Corporation. Name the company ________.
35. Which is the oldest Foreign Bank in India?

36. C.K. Ranganathan founder of Cavin Kare observed that rural consumers continued to use soaps to wash their hair. What was his action that completely shook P&G and HLL?
37. Which was the first detergent powder to be marketed in India?
38. Which was India's first detergent cake?
39. Which is the world's first operational nuclear powered submarine?
40. Which company designed and manufactured the first anti-theft car stereo-receiver?
41. Which airlines holds the world record for the maximum people embarked on a single aircraft when it evacuated 673 people on a single 747 Boeing flight during Cyclone Tracy?
42. Which is the first airline to install hospital grade air filter True HEPA capable of intercepting 99.99 per cent dust particles and microorganisms on every flight?
43. Which hotel was commissioned by Tata Group founder Jamsetji Nusserwanji Tata after he was refused entry to the now defunct Apollo Hotel, which had a strict Europeans – only policy?
44. Where is the world's first Armani Hotel to be located?
45. When was the hot air balloon first used for military purpose?
46. Who introduced the first automatic washing machine?
47. Which company's AC alternator was used to power the world's first electric streetlighting in the town of Godalming, United Kingdom?
48. Where is India's first centrally air-conditioned bus terminal coming up?
49. What is the number of branches added to ICICI Bank by the acquisition of Bank of Madura (2001), Sangli Bank (2007) and Bank of Rajasthan (2010)?
50. Where was the first ever distillation plant in the country to produce Extra Neutral Alcohol commissioned?
51. Where is the world's first gold dispensing ATM installed?
52. Who overtook South Africa which was on top for 101 years in 2007 as the world's leading producer of gold?
53. Who robbed the Louvre, the world's most famous museum, of Leonardo da Vinci's Mono Lisa in 1911?
54. Who was the first woman to run a nationally prominent newspaper in the United States?
55. Which is India's largest amusement park?
56. Which was the first airliner to have a fly by wire flight control system?
57. Who supplied portable toilets for Beijing Olympics?

58. Which is the world's tallest skyscraper?
59. Which is Hollywood's first trade magazine?
60. Which is the largest diamond ever discovered?
61. Who brought color television transmission to India with the supply of four outdoor broadcast vans to Doordarshan during the IX Asian Games in 1982?
62. The world's first quartz watch was made by _________.
63. Which is the first Public Sector Bank to start the concept of branchless banking in India?
64. What is the world's smallest gaming laptop that was launched by Dell and Allenware?
65. What was famous about the Alto bearing chasis number 1126046?
66. Which club's home ground Bootham Crescent was renamed Kit Kat Crescent after the same was sponsored by Nestle Rowntree?
67. What is the name of India's longest rail bridge which is located in Kochin?
68. Which business model did Four Season's Hotel chain adopt after cost overrun at its Vancouver property almost led it to bankruptcy?
69. Who was the first US brewer to use pasteurization to keep beer fresh?
70. Which is the first organization to mass produce visible LED by using gallium arsenide phosphide which produces red LEDs suitable for indicators?
71. Which company gave Rudolf Diesel the opportunity to test and develop his ideas and build a working engine according to his theory and design which is now emphasized in the print advertisement of the company?
72. The academy of motion picture Arts and Science was established in 1927 and instantly set about devising a trophy to honour outstanding achievement in film. MGM's chief art director Cedric Gibbons and Los Angeles sculptor George Stanley were commissioned to design the statuette in the form of a knight standing on a reel of film, his hands gripping his sword and the statuette is 13.5 inches tall and weighs 8.5 lbs, and made of gold plated britannium metal. Name the award –
73. Which is the first company in Asia to produce recombinant human insulin?
74. Which company launched the *'spirit of India'* limited edition USB flash drives exclusively for the Indian market?
75. Which is the first Indian entity to obtain sound mark registration for its corporate jingle, which goes "Dhin Chik Dhin Chik"?

76. India's first museum dedicated to contraband goods seized by the customs and excise department of the Government of India is situated in ________.
77. India's first government controlled religious bank is being launched by ________.
78. The world's largest stroller making group is ________.
79. Which is the first Indian company to operate an airport outside the country?
80. Which company has launched the world's smallest *Bhagvad Gita* in 24 karat gold?
81. Which is the first railway project in the world to claim carbon credits?
82. Name the organization that has entered the Guiness Book of World Records by planting 1,25,256 saplings in a record time of 6 hrs. 35 minutes, involving 1,400 volunteers ________.
83. Which was India's first non-banking finance company to launch a global credit card?
84. Which company changed the colour of its bottle crowns to red, white and blue in support of America's war effort and ran a canteen in Times Square that enabled millions to record messages for armed services personnel?
85. Which is the oldest watch manufacturer in the world with an uninterrupted history and whose clients include Napoleon Bonaparte, Pope Pius X1 and Duke of Windsor?
86. Which is the first mass production car company outside the USA?
87. Which is the world's highest restaurant?
88. Which is the first Indian media organization to create an ipad application?
89. Which company developed the world's first Internet mobile messaging platform?
90. Which is the world's first company to issue the Travellers' cheque?
91. Under which Act the government rejected the Montblac's plea for using Gandhiji's image in limited edition pens?
92. Which airways pioneered live cooking when airborne?
93. When was the movement "Quit Facebook Day" where a number of users around the globe planned to delete their Facebook profiles in protest over recent privacy issues on the world's largest social network?
94. Which was the first small goods carrier on four-wheels to be launched in India to facilitate last mile distribution in a market that was dominated by three-wheeled commercial vehicles?

95. Which is the first feature-length dramatic film made especially for three-dimensional projections?
96. Which company created the world's first vertical oval shaped bath fittings?
97. Which company was the first manufacturer of videogames?
98. Which company manufactures the largest number of laptops in the world?
99. Which is considered as a 'Goan Treasure' that is seeking international exposure and has made Goa to participate at the prestigious International Spirits Challenge 2009 (ISC) event in London?
100. Which company was India's maiden, free internet service provider?
101. This was the first post-deregulation airline company, launched in India in 1993, by a partnership deal with German carrier – Lufthansa. The company faced bankruptcy and ceased its operations in 1996. Using its Air Operating Certificate (AOC) it was reincarnated as Royal Airways and later renamed as SpiceJet in 2005. Name the company –
102. Which is the world's largest syringe manufacturer?
103. Which company has the distinction of manufacturing first in India 'scissor cross over' for Bangalore Metro that allows the train to go to any of the multiple tracks at that point?
104. Which company entered the Guiness Book of World Records in 1987 as the largest manufacturer of bicycles?
105. Which company manufactured the first dashboard installed car radios?

Answers

1. Sydney
2. India
3. Sarong Kebaya
4. The World Bank and International Monetary Fund
5. Bernard Ghillebaert, Friedhelm Hillebrand and Oculy Silaban
6. Xerox
7. The Mangala processing terminal of Cairn Energy which is 670 km. long
8. Kochi
9. To emphasize the importance of product quality
10. Father's Day

11. The Mall of India being built by DLF Universal on NH-8 highway on Delhi-Gurgaon border and will cover an area of 45,00,000 square foot.
12. It will stick to emerging markets in three regions (Asia, Africa and Latin America) and in three categories: personal care, hair care and insecticides.
13. McLeod Russell the world's largest tea producer producing approximately 100 million kgs. a year from tea estates in West Bengal, Assam, Vietnam and Uganda.
14. Mahindra
15. The Milan based Luxottica Group. Its portfolio includes house brands such as Oakley, Inc, Revo, Arnette, Killer Loop, Persol, Vogue, Luxxotica and Sferoflex.
16. Lord Venkateswara, the presiding deity at the Tirumala temple in Thirupathi. A policy framed at the instance of the Japanese Company prohibited the company from making donations. The decision to donate a car to the deity at Tirupathi was taken by vendors, dealers and employees who paid for the car.
17. SKS Microfinance
18. United Way
19. Unitech's Great India Place at Noida with an area of 15,00,000 sq. ft.
20. It was a collaboration with Carl Zeiss which resulted in the new, professional 35 mm SLR with an electronically-controlled shutter bearing the Contax name.
21. Century Plyboards India
22. Singapore Girl of Singapore Airlines
23. The Coconut Development Board
24. The United States and India
25. Ansco logoed Minolta Hi Matic Camera
26. Casio
27. Wipro
28. Stripe
29. The Raintree Hotel in Mount Road, Chennai
30. ITC Royal Gardenia, Bangalore
31. It was founded in 2000 by a group of telecom industry insiders in Helsinki (Nokia Country) who would meet every Monday to discuss trends in the industry. All MoMo meetings are open to general public
32. Rediff.com
33. The MCard for ₹ 499 which offers one million minutes of talk time valid for 20 years

34. I-flex
35. Standard Chartered Bank set-up in 1806
36. 50 P Chik Shampoo sachets when other shampoo sachets were selling at ₹ 2
37. Surf detergent powder marketed by Levers since 1959
38. Bonus from TOMCO
39. USS Nautilus. It was so named after the submarine in Jules Verne's 'Twenty thousand Leagues under the sea'
40. Kenwood
41. Qantas
42. Thai Airways
43. Taj Mahal Palace
44. The bottom 39 floors of Bhurj Khalifa skyscraper in Dubai
45. Battle of Fleurus, where the balloon l'Entreprenant was used as an observation post
46. Bendix
47. Siemens
48. Mohali, the project is being carried out by C&C
49. 263, 198 and 463 respectively
50. Cherthala (Bottled Beehive French Brandy for Herbertsons Limited)
51. Emirates Palace Hotel, Abu Dhabi on May 12, 2010
52. China
53. Italian immigrant Vincenzo Peruggia. He claimed that his patriotism drove him to return the painting to Italy his motherland.
54. Katharine Graham
55. 'Wonder La'
56. Concorde
57. Sintex Industries the largest plastic manufacturer in India together with Poly John International.
58. Burj Dubai
59. The Hollywood Reporter
60. The 'Cullinan Diamond'
61. Philips
62. Seiko (Seiko Quartz Astron 35 SQ)
63. Corporation Bank
64. M11x
65. It was the millionth Alto

66. York City F.C.
67. Vembanad Bridge
68. Management only business model – operating on behalf of real estate owners and developers.
69. Adolphus Busch
70. Monsanto
71. MAN AG
72. Oscar
73. Wockhardt
74. Transcend
75. ICICI
76. Goa
77. Kerala Government
78. Goodbaby Group
79. GMR
80. Tanishq
81. Delhi Metro
82. Sahara Amby Valley Project
83. Tata Finance
84. Pepsi
85. Vacheron Constantin
86. Citroen
87. Atmosphere situated at Burj Khalifa in Dubai
88. Mint
89. Unimobile.
90. American Express in 1891
91. Emblems and Names (Prevention of Improper Use) Act, 1959
92. Cathay Pacific
93. May 31st 2010
94. Ace by Tata Motors
95. Bwana Devil (1952) Director-Oboler
96. Karatoer from Jaguar
97. Atari
98. Lenora from Taiwan
99. Feni made from Coconut and Cashew Apple
100. Caltiger.com

101. ModiLuft founded by the Indian Industrialist S.K. Modi
102. Becht & Dickinson
103. Mazda Concrete Products Plant at Tumkur
104. Hero Cycles
105. Delco

Section – II

10. Kids
11. Sports
12. Auto
13. Maritime

Questions

1. Which popular television channel was called Pinwheel when it debuted in 1977?
2. What is the name of the 10.5 inch fashion doll, originally called Takara Barbie, produced by Japanese toy manufacturing company Takara?
3. What is the name of the robotic toy being launched by Air Robot India, a part of the Chennai based Mandot Group?
4. Which is the first ever Fischer Price toy that was sold?
5. Which Japanese company created the Dollfie brand of vinyl dolls in 1997?
6. Which social networking site aimed at 6 to 10-year-old children and founded by Mandeep Dhillon was bought by Walt Disney Company?
7. Who is dubbed as the 'Father of the Play Station'?
8. Which toy company produces the line of action figure G. I. Joe?
9. What is the name of toy Jenny's boy friend, manufactured by the toy company Takara?
10. Who created the American animated television series Dora the Explorer?
11. What is the tile based game for two to four players invented by Ephraim Hertzano a Romanian born Jew?
12. Who was the creator of the Bratz range of dolls that gave serious competition to Barbie in the fashion doll market?
13. What is the name of the range of dolls introduced by MGA Entertainment intended as a replacement for Bratz doll?
14. What is peculiar with the doll 'share a smile Becky' introduced by Mattel in May 1997?
15. What is the name of the German doll that was Ruth Handler's inspiration in the creation of Barbie?

16. Which company introduced the Sonny and Cher line of 12.5 inch celebrity dolls to compete with Mattel's Barbie dolls?
17. What is the name of the company that was started in 1994 as 'Todd Toys' by Todd Mcfarlane but whose name was changed due to pressure from Mattel?
18. What is the name of the robotic line of toys initiated by Lego in 1998?
19. What was established by Cornish William in London in 1970?
20. What is the name of the toy brand for pre-schoolers, originally produced by Fischer-Price in the 1960s as the play family?
21. Which doll was created in 2001 by a Japanese software company called Petworks?
22. Which company created the original Mickey Mouse watch for Disney in 1914?
23. If Play-station is to Sony Wii is to ________.
24. Who started children's supermarket which later evolved into the modern day 'Toys R U' retail chain?
25. Which toy company was started by David Abrams that was known prior to 1971 as a producer of dime store toys?
26. Who is the Japanese maker of Transformers and Pokeman toys?
27. Which German toy company's Indian arm has got the exclusive license to manufacture and merchandise the official mascot of cricket World Cup 2011, for two consecutive years?
28. Name the initiative launched by Nick to bring global issues to children's doorsteps.
29. Which was the first Fischer-Price toy to make use of plastic?
30. Theodor Friedrich Wilhelm started a tin plate Toy Company in Goppingen in 1859. Theodor died seven years later and his wife Caroline ran the business until 1888 when her sons Eugen and Karl tookover. They presented the world's first standardized-track toy train at the Leipzig fair in 1891. Six years later they launched the world's first electric toy train. In 1935 they came out with the first miniature electric railway. Its products have been called "the kings of trains and the trains of kings". Identify the company.
31. Which company is credited with Zaxxon, the first game to employ axonometric projection and Hang-on, the world's first full body experience videogame?
32. Who makes the Angry Birds game?
33. Who is credited with making the M Quarks game which unlike traditional stick based construction sets uses M Quarks which resemble

golf balls that lock onto one another with magnets and can even be used to learn Physics, electricity and magnetism?

34. Which company released the submarine simulator game 'Periscope'?
35. Who is the first Bollywood actress to be likened to the iconic Barbie doll and joins an exclusive list of celebrities such as Julie Andrews, Audrey Hepburn, Barbara Streisand, Marilyn Monroe and others who have been part of the Barbie family since 1967?
36. The popular toys like Ultra Machine and Kousenjuu were produced by ________.
37. China's bead toys are sold in the US under the brand of ________.
38. What is the acronym MGM, the studio that produces famous Tom & Jerry Cartoon stand for?

Answers

1. Nickelodeon
2. Jenny
3. Ringbo, India's first commercial riding robot to be sold as a toy is a small car for five year olds. Mandot has a tie-up with Sri Lanka's Techno Innovations Pvt. Ltd., to market Ringbo and its successors.
4. Dr. Doodle in 1931
5. Volks
6. Togetherville
7. Ken Kutaragi
8. Hasbro
9. Jeff
10. Chris Gifford, Valerie Walsh and Eric Weiner
11. Rummikub
12. Carter Bryant
13. Moxie Girlz
14. It is a doll in a pink wheel chair
15. Bild Lilli
16. Mego Corporation
17. McFarlane Toys
18. Mindstorms
19. Hamleys, a world famous toy retailer
20. Little People
21. Momoko doll

22. Timex
23. Nintendo
24. Charles Lazarus
25. Mego Corporation
26. Tomy Co.
27. German Toy giant Simba Dickie Group's Indian Arm Simba Toys
28. The Big Green Help
29. Buzzy Bee
30. Marklin – the world's oldest, largest and finest toy and model train manufacturer.
31. Sega
32. Rovio Mobile
33. Francisco Pacheco Kitzing from Costa Rica
34. Sega Enterprises
35. Katrina Kaif
36. Nintendo
37. Aqua Dots
38. Metro Goldwyn Mayer

Questions

1. Who started the sports goods firm Adidas?
2. Which company introduced 'White Line' collection, the first range of coloured apparel in the history of tennis?
3. Which swimwear did Michael Phelp wear in the Beijing Olympics?
4. What is the present name of the company started as Humphreys Brothers Clothing in 1919 in Cheshire?
5. Which sports company bought over Umbro in the year 2007?
6. Which is claimed as the first performance basket ball shoe that has been created from manufacturing waste?
7. What is the name of the company founded in January 1964 that we know now as Nike?
8. Who are the founders of Nike?
9. For which Japanese shoe maker did Blue Ribbon Sport initially operate as a distributor?
10. Who was the founder of ASICS?
11. ASICS is an acronym of the Latin phrase "anima sana in corpore sano". What does it mean?
12. Who founded Lacoste, a high end apparel company in 1933?
13. Which company is recognized by its green crocodile Logo with the crocodile facing to the right?
14. Which company was founded by Joseph William Foster in 1895 along with his adult sons after he came up with the novel idea of a spiked running shoe?
15. How was the name Reebok (1960) chosen?
16. Who founded Yonex?
17. Which sports equipment manufacturing company that originated in Annecy France was started by Francois, his wife and son?

18. Which is the first ever production shoe to use a microprocessor?
19. In 2001, with whom did Sachin Tendulkar sign a five-year contract worth ₹ 100 crore?
20. Who was the first manufacturer to offer sports shoes with Velcro Fasteners?
21. Which cricketer has co-created a toothpaste with the Future group with the tagline, 'Ab din ki shurvat, sach se!'?
22. He was the skipper of Indian Hockey team having won Indian colours for eight years in 180 international matches including Athens Olympics and World Cup. He later did his MBA at ISB, Hyderabad and became the CEO of Olympic Gold Quest, not for profit organization that bridges the gap between India's best athletes and the best in the world. Identify the personality ________.
23. Which shoe manufacturer was the sponsor of Jamaican track athlete Usain Bolt who won three gold medals by breaking the men's 100m, 200m and 4 × 100m world record in 2008 Beijing Olympics?
24. For the New Delhi Common Wealth Games 272 gold, 272 silver and 282 bronze medals are to be given to athletes. The cost of producing a gold medal is ₹ 5,539, a silver medal ₹ 4,818 and a bronze medal ₹ 4,529. The lanyard of the medal carries all six game colours (pink, purple, green, red, yellow and blue) blending into each other. Where are they manufactured?
25. India is the largest manufacturer and exporter of cricket bats in the world. Which chemical used for the treatment of English willows (imported mainly from UK and used in the manufacture of cricket bats) has been banned by the European Union?
26. Which brand of boots scored the maximum number of goals during the FIFA 2010 World Cup?
27. The winning gold of the FIFA 2010 finals was scored by a ____________ branded boot
28. Who started the sports goods firm Puma?

Answers

1. Adolf Dasler
2. Fila
3. Speedo LZR. It is ultrasonically stitched together and mimics the surface of fish. Its fit is so snug that it can take 20-30 minutes just to get into one
4. Umbro
5. Nike

6. The trash talk shoe from Nike
7. Blue Ribbon Sports
8. Philip Knight and Bill Bowerman
9. Onitsuka Tiger
10. Kihachiro Onitsuka
11. A sound mind in a sound body
12. Rene Lacoste and Andre Gillier
13. Lacoste
14. Reebok, then Foster and Sons
15. African spelling of Rhebok, a type of African antelope or gazelle
16. Minoru Yoneyama
17. Salomon Group
18. Adidas 1. Dubbed by the company the world's first intelligent shoe, it features a microprocessor capable of performing 5 million calculations per second that automatically adjusts the shoe's level of cushioning to suit its environment.
19. WorldTel
20. Puma
21. Sachin Tendulkar
22. Viren Rasquinho
23. Puma
24. The Government Mint, Kolkata.
25. Methyl Bromide
26. F50 Adizero from Adidas
27. Nike
28. Rudolf Dasler

12 AUTO

Questions

1. Which company made the trials bike Sherpa T?
2. Which was the first manufacturer to implement four-wheel drive technology into series car production?
3. What is the name of the two-wheeler manufactured by Mopeds India Ltd., started by Coimbatore based Textile Group VLB?
4. Ferdinando Innocenti, whose pre-war metal tubing business Innocenti had been damaged during World War II, asked General Corradino D'Ascanio, who was responsibl e for designing the modern helicopter, to design an affordable means of transport to the masses. When the vehicle was designed, D'Ascanio had designed it on a moulded and beaten spar-frame, whereas Innocenti wanted the frame from rolled tubing as he also wanted to revive his other pre-war business. Hence D'Ascanio dissociated from Innocenti and took the design to Enrico Piaggio, whose fighter plane factory was demolished in war bombing and started manufacturing this product. Identify the name of the vehicle ________.
5. Which Indian company acquired the entire production line of Puch Maxi Plus when production was stopped in Austria?
6. Which Chinese auto giant has acquired Volvo, the Swedish automaker, owned by Ford, making it the biggest acquisition of an overseas company by a Chinese company?
7. Which is the first manufacturer to introduce turn signals in cars?
8. Which company acquired Ssangyang Motors in 1998 but sold it in 2000 after it ran into financial trouble?
9. What is the name of the passenger car division started by Swedish Airplane Limited?
10. Which truck manufacturing company's name was Manhattan before the same was changed to the family name of the founders?
11. Who founded the Italian motorcycle company Aprilia?

12. In which vehicle did Audrey Hepburn Side saddle with Gregory Peck in the Hollywood film *Roman Holiday* for a ride through Rome which resulted in that particular vehicle selling 1,00,000 units?
13. Which company produced bikes for the American market under the brand, 'American Eagle'?
14. Which company pioneered equal sized front and rear wheels for its cycles with pneumatic tyres?
15. Which company started by brother's Charles and Fred, was acquired by Tube Investments in the 1950s?
16. Which motorcycle did Frantisek Janecek manufacture after he bought the motorcycle division of Wanderer in 1929?
17. Who launched India's first taxi jingles and announcement system on July 23, 2004?
18. What is the name of the globally benchmarked pre-owned car programme launched by Mercedes Benz?
19. Ferdinando Innocenti, whose pre-war seamless steel tubing business Innocenti had been damaged during World War II wanted to design an affordable means of private transport to the masses. He also wanted to revive his metal tubing business. After overcoming production difficulties through his choice of tubular frame he started producing a vehicle. Identify the vehicle ________.
20. Which is the car with the twin kidney shaped grill on its face and the blue and white Logo atop the hood?
21. The first Mercedes Benz brand name vehicles were produced in 1926 by the merger of two companies. Whose companies are they?
22. Which company advertises its product as the 'First safe School Bus' to be made in India and first developed in 1996, designed in association with Institute of Road Traffic Education and IIT, Delhi?
23. Which company sued Mahindra for allegedly copying the design of its vehicle for the front grill of Mahindra Scorpio?
24. Which is the first automobile manufacturer to build air-conditioner into its cars?
25. On which model was the Premier Padmini that was built in India between 1968 and 2000 by Premier Automobiles based?
26. Which is the largest selling truck model worldwide?
27. Which is the first Indian car to have a fibre glass body and was launched by Bangalore based Sipani Automobiles in 1978?
28. TVS has designed a bike to carry heavy loads across long distances with 4 shock absorbers, detachable rear seat to accommodate goods, big brakes, an easy centre stand, long wheel base and wider tyres. What is the name of the bike?

29. What was the name of the badge engineered version of Tata Indica that was imported and sold in UK?
30. On which model is the Ambassador car made by Hindustan Motors based on?
31. Which model other than Model T from Ford's stable was produced only in black colour?
32. Along with whom did Mercedes Benz produce a limited edition sports car?
33. Which car is the hero of the film Herbie: Fully Loaded?
34. What was the name of this company when it was finally acquired by General Motors, which was established as National Motors in 1937 and later in early 60s named as Saenara Motors?
35. With whom did Louis Chevrolet, a leading race car driver join hands to form the Chevrolet Motor car company in 1909?
36. What is the name of the Automobile manufacturing division of the Japanese conglomerate Fiji Heavy Industries?
37. What is the name of the car that was launched by Chevrolet as an answer to Ford's Model T in 1917?
38. Which is the first car company to use Aluminium to create an entire car frame by the inspiration of the branched structure of an insect's wing with the belief that lighter can be stronger?
39. Why was the Bultaco Motorcycle Company so named?
40. American Academy of Hospitality Services presents a prestigious award worldwide for top luxury hotels, restaurants and cruise ships. In the year 2010, the award was conferred to a high-end luxury car for 'perfectly encapsulating a sense of fascination and legend'. Name the car marque.
41. Which is considered as the world's first SUV?
42. What is the name of the branded membership based two-wheeler rental services for the urban commuter started by Electrotherm the manufacturers of YoByke?
43. What is the name of the first ever transporter model that was used as a panel van for goods and passengers and whose manufacturing was started in Wolfsburg in 1950?
44. Which is the first series produced car in the world to cover 100 kilometres on just 3 litres of diesel?
45. Who pioneered the technology of Anti-lock Braking System (ABS) for motorcycles in 1988?
46. Which was the first motorcycle to offer test rides during exhibition shows?

Answers

1. Bultaco
2. Audi
3. Suvega
4. Vespa
5. Hero Motors
6. Geely
7. Buick
8. Daewoo Motors
9. SAAB (Svenska Aeroplan Aktiebolaget)
10. Mack Trucks
11. Cavaliere Alberto
12. Vespa
13. Laverda
14. F.I.V. Edoardo Bianchi
15. Norman Cycles
16. Jawa which was the first two letters of Janacek and Wanderer
17. The 8,000 cab strong Bengal taxi association to minimize losses stemming from passenger forgetfulness.
18. Proven Exclusivity
19. Lambretta
20. BMW
21. Karl Benz and Gottlieb Daimler's Companies
22. Eicher Skyline
23. Chrysler
24. Packard Motor Car Company
25. Fiat 1100
26. Actros from Mercedes Benz
27. Dolphin
28. TVS Max 4R
29. Rover CityRover
30. Morris Oxford III made by Morris Motor Company at Oxford from 1956 to 1959
31. Lincoln
32. McLaren Cars
33. Beetle

34. Daewoo
35. William Durant, the founder of General Motors
36. Subaru
37. 490 (Named so to reflect its dollar price)
38. Audi
39. The first four letters are based on the founder's name 'Francisco Bulto' while the last three letters are from his nick name 'Paco'.
40. Maybach
41. Suburban Carryall from Chevrolet
42. Switch
43. Bully
44. Lupo 3L TDI
45. BMW Motorrad
46. Jawa

Questions

1. What does the P&O in P&O Nedlloyd which was acquired by Maersk Group in 2006, earlier the second largest door-to-door container shipping company in the world connecting more than 250 main ports and a larger number of smaller ones through an extensive feeder network, stand for?
2. Identify the familiar media baron who was born Jan Ludwik Hoch and died under mysterious circumstances aboard his yacht 'Lady Ghislaine'.
3. Aviation turned sailor Sir Francis Chichester completed his voyage in this yacht in a record 107 days in 1967. In 2004., The UK sailing academy bought it from the dock for $ 1 and a gin and tonic. It set sail once more in 2005, carrying a crew of young adults with disadvantaged backgrounds. What is the name of this yacht?
4. Which is the largest container ship in the world?
5. What is the name of arms dealer Adnan Khashoggi's yacht which was built in 1980 and which at that time was the world's largest yacht, measuring 281 feet?
6. This yacht can sail across the Atlantic Ocean in just ten days. Originally built for American business man Tom Perkins, it was bought by millionairess Elena Ambrosiadou. What is its name?
7. Which Indian business man owns the yacht Indian Princess?
8. The largest yacht in the world belongs to Russian oil magnate Roman Abramovich. It has two helipads, a submarine and a military grade missile detection system. What is the name of this yacht?
9. Who in an attempt to end the World War I chartered a peace ship to take 170 peace leaders to Europe in 1915, the event being the centre of the novel titled, King Henry by Douglas Galbraith?
10. Which is the world's largest lessor of intermodal containers?

11. Adnan Khashoggi's yacht featured in the James Bond movie, *Never Say Never Again.* The boat has changed many hands and at present belongs to a Saudi business man. What is its present name?
12. Identify the ₹ 100 crore company Malav Shroff a medical practitioner and Sujat Chohan former country director Gartner Inc. joined to form, that sells leisure power boats and yachts through imports. They pioneered the Mumbai International Boat Show 2007 and edited India's first luxury boating magazine *India Boating*.
13. This 325 foot yacht was Onassis's headquarters. This boat hosted the reception to two famous weddings – Prince Rainier to Grace Kelly and Onassis to Jackie Kennedy. What is its name?
14. Who was the former prime minister and media tycoon who chartered a yacht called 'Excellent' to conduct his election campaign?
15. This was originally a 1939 Boeing 307 Stratoliner airplane owned by Howard Hughes. In 1964, it suffered massive damage from Hurricane Cleo, and was soon declared abandoned property. It was bought for $ 62 in an auction, turned into a boat and currently owned by David Drimmer. What is its present name?
16. Who has promoted ABG shipyard, India's largest private ship builder?
17. What was the name of the yacht owned by Thomas Lipton that took part in 1899, America's cup race?
18. Which is the largest container ship operator and supply vessel operator in the world?
19. What is the name of the joint venture between the Mahindra Group and Ocean Blue, situated at the Pilerne Industrial Estate, to manufacture fibreglass powerboats?
20. Which is Independent India's first indigenous steamship?
21. National Maritime Day is celebrated on 5th April to commemorate –
22. Which is the largest seller of second hand containers in the world?
23. What is the name of the first Swadeshi ship launched by V.O. Chidambaram Pillai in 1906 from Tuticorin Harbour?
24. Which company designed the then world's largest floating crane in 1910, which was designed for Harlland & Wolff in Belfast which was used for building RMS Titanic?

Answers

1. Peninsular and Oriental
2. Robert Maxwell
3. Gipsy Moth IV
4. Emma Maersk

5. Nubila, his daughters name
6. Maltese Falcon
7. Vijay Mallya
8. Eclipse
9. Henry Ford, the group went to neutral Sweden and the Netherlands to meet with peace activists.
10. Textainer
11. Kingdom 5KR
12. Ocean Blue
13. Christina O (Named by Aristotle Onassis after his daughter Christina)
14. Silvio Berlusconi
15. Cosmic Muffin
16. Rishi Agarwal
17. Shamrock
18. A.P. Moller – Maersk Group based in Copenhagen, Denmark
19. Mahindra Odyessea
20. Jal-Usha, the 8,000 tons maiden vessel of Scindia Shipyard
21. The voyage of the first Indian ship S.S. Loyalty from Mumbai to London on 5th April, 1919
22. Textainer
23. S.S. Gaelia
24. Demag Cranes

Section – III

14. Terms and Acronyms
15. Books
16. Slogan
17. Mascots
18. Logos
19. Company's and Brand's Logos

Questions

1. What is the Baltic Dry Index?
2. What are teaser rates?
3. What is Salmon day?
4. What is Rugmark?
5. Who introduced the market segmentation concept in his 1956 article, 'Product Differentiation and Market Segmentation as an Alternative Marketing Strategy'?
6. For what purpose was Technology Upgradation Fund Scheme (TUFS) launched in 1999?
7. What type of an advertisement according to Ogilvy is a 'headless wonder'?
8. Who was the Indian who coined the term 'Core Competency' along with Gary Hamel?
9. What's the term used for adding non-essential features to make a product more appealing than it is?
10. Which company has launched a strategy termed "Supplier of choice"?
11. Who proposed Unique Selling Propostion (USP)?
12. What is a Bridge in Television commercial?
13. What is Dematerialisation?
14. What does 'Theory I Management' refer to?
15. What is the term for just-in-time inventory control, named after Japanese word for the control cards used in JIT?
16. What is 'Grape Escapade festival'?
17. What does the acronym ESPN stand for?
18. What does the acronym MAN a German truck major stand for?
19. What does the acronym SLR (in SLR Camera) stand for?
20. What does the acronym BARC stand for?

21. What does the acronym TAM stand for?
22. What does the acronym BMW stand for?
23. What does the EID acronym in EID Parry Ltd., the flagship of Murugappa Group stand for?
24. What does the name REVA (The electric car project in Bangalore) stand for?
25. NASDAQ is an acronym for ________.
26. What does the acronym CIBIL stand for, which came into being in 2004 – the stakeholders being State Bank of India, Housing Development Finance Corporation Limited, Dun & Bradstreet Information Services India Pvt. Ltd., and Trans Union International Inc. in the proportion of 40:40:10:10?
27. What does the acronym DELCO in DELCO Electronics Corporation stand for?
28. What does the acronym NCDEX – which offers futures trading in 47 commodities in agriculture, energy, metals, plastics and carbon credits stand for?
29. What does acronym Viacom stand for, Viacom being a United States media conglomerate with interests in cinema and cable television?
30. What does the acronym POSCO, a large Asian steel maker stand for?
31. Expand ANDA ________.
32. Monsanto's corn and cotton seeds containing genes for pest killing toxins coded Bt. What does the Bt stand for?
33. What is TGV, in TGV train stand for?
34. What does the acronym YAHOO denote?
35. What does the acronym WIPRO stand for?
36. Expand SATA, an acronym based on computer hard drives ________.

Answers

1. Tracks worldwide prices of dry-bulk maritime cargo since 1985
2. It is an introductory loan scheme offering attractive fixed interest rates for a short duration on home/car loans, the fixed interest rate under the scheme – is much below market rate – turns floating at the end of the scheme period
3. A day spent making a lot of effort to achieve something but getting nowhere in the end
4. It stood for hand knotted carpets which were not made by employing child labour
5. Wendel Smith
6. To provide interest subsidy for modernization of textile mills

7. An advertising without a headline; Ogilvy says that since the headline more than anything else will decide the success of an advertisement, it is a silly thing indeed to have an advertisement without a headline.
8. C.K. Prahalad
9. Bells and Whistles
10. De Beers by establishing globally recognized distribution channels
11. Roser Reeves
12. Transition from one scene to another
13. Holding and trading securities in paperless mode (Demat)
14. India-centric Management, by Arindam Chaudhuri
15. Kanban
16. Wine and Haute Cuisine festival organized by Goa Tourism Development Corporation Ltd., (GTDC) every year since 2005 with the aim of promoting tourism activities in Goa
17. Entertainment and Sports Programming Network
18. Maschinenfabrik Augsburg-Numberg AG
19. Single-Lens Reflex
20. Broadcast Audio Research Council
21. Television Audio Measurement
22. Bayerische Motoren Werke
23. East India Distilleries
24. Revolutionary Electric Vehicle Alternative
25. National Association of Securities Dealers Automated Quotations
26. Credit Information Bureau of India Ltd.
27. Dayton Engineering Laboratories Co.
28. National Commodity and Derivatives Exchange Ltd.
29. Video Audio Communications
30. Pohang Iron and Steel Company
31. Abbreviated New Drug Applications
32. Bacillus Thuringiensis
33. Train a la Grande Vitesse, currently operated by SNCF, the French National rail operator.
34. Yet Another Hierarchical Officious Oracle
35. West Indian Vegetable Products Ltd.
36. Serial Advanced Technology Attachment

❀ ❀ ❀

Questions

1. Who wrote the book *'Wealth of Nations'* in 1776?
2. Who wrote the book *'Predictably Irrational'*?
3. Who wrote the book *'Bankruptcy to Billions'*, chronicling Lalu's feat as railway minister?
4. 'It happened in India' is the autobiography of ________.
5. 'Beyond the last blue Mountain' is the title of the autobiography of ________.
6. 'Brushes with History' is the autobiography of ________.
7. 'When You Care Enough' is the autobiography of ________.
8. Who is the author of the book *'The Ranbaxy Story'*?
9. Who wrote the book *'Bangalore Tiger'*?
10. Who wrote the book, *'Fighting the Corporation: The Hoover Flight Fiasco'*, based on a promotional offer which went awry?
11. Soros: The life and times of a messianic billionaire was written by ________.
12. 'No Mere Bagatelles' written by Jeffrey Sussman is the biography of ________.
13. What is the relationship between Gulliver's Travel and Microfinance institution?
14. Who authored the book, *'Global Crisis, Recession and Uneven Recovery'*?
15. What is the name of the hundred page magazine, designed for the iPad, which was launched by Apple and News Corp.?
16. Whose autobiography is 'Stop and Sell the Roses'?
17. Who wrote the book *'You can have it all'*?
18. Which airline's experiences were turned into a child's book Gum Wrappers and Goggles by Winifred Barnum in 1983?

19. 'Practical Wisdom ...in real life and management', is a book written by ________.
20. Who authored the book, *'Barbarians at the Gate: The Fall of RJR Nabisco'*, based on a series of articles written by the authors for *Wall Street Journal* and which was later made into a television movie by HBO?
21. Which best seller by Ricardo Semler is based on his experience with Brazilian company SEMCO?
22. "Who says elephants can't dance" is a book about the historic turnaround of which company?
23. Whose autobiography is titled 'Be my Guest'?
24. Whose autobiography is titled 'Beyond Boundaries'?
25. Whose autobiography is known as *'Work-in-progress'*?
26. Whose biography is titled 'The Snow Ball'?
27. Who is the author of the book *'Launching India: Ideas for the new Century'*?
28. Who wrote the book *'Every street paved with Gold'*?
29. Who are the authors of the international best-seller 'Winning'?
30. Who are the authors of the book, *'The HR Scorecard – Linking People, Strategy and Performance'*?
31. Who wrote 'Balanced Scorecard – Translating Strategy into Action'?
32. Who is the author of the world famous book on branding *'Brand Warfare'*?
33. Stay Hungry, Stay Foolish which features stories of 25 MBAs, who left lucrative jobs to become entrepreneurs was authored by
34. *'Father, Son & Co.'* is a book written by –
35. Jagran Prakashan in 2007 launched a Hinglish newspaper named ________.
36. What is the name of the annual newsletter that is published by Microsoft?
37. At 17, he became a lay preacher but soon joined Bissell Carpet Sweeper Company. At 41, he was hired by Albert Lasker to write copy for Lord & Thomas. He created campaigns for Pepsodent, Palmolive and six different cars. He is the author of the book *'Scientific Advertising'*. Identify the personality ________.

Answers

1. Adam Smith
2. Dan Ariely
3. Sudhir Kumar a Bihar cadre IAS officer of 1982 batch
4. Kishore Biyani

5. JRD Tata
6. Krishna Kumar Birla
7. Joyce C. Hall
8. Bhupesh Bhandari
9. Steve Hamm
10. Harry E. Cichy
11. Michael T. Kaufman
12. Judith Leiber and her husband Gerson Leiber
13. Jonathan Swift who wrote the Lilliput story started what is considered as the first MFI, the Irish Loan Fund with a contribution of £ 500 to provide loans without collateral to the poor of Dublin
14. Y.V. Reddy, former Governor of Reserve Bank of India
15. The Daily
16. James F. McCann
17. Mary Kay Ash
18. South West Airlines
19. Kochouseph Chittilappilly
20. Bryan Burrough and John Helyar
21. Maverick
22. IBM
23. Conrad Hilton
24. Lord Swaraj Paul
25. Michael Eisner of Disney
26. Warren Buffet
27. Nandan Nilekani
28. Kim Woo Jung, who founded the Daewoo Group in 1967
29. Jack Welch and Suzy Welch
30. D. Ulrich, B.E. Becker and M.A. Huselid
31. Kaplan and Norton
32. David F. D'Alessandro
33. Rashmi Bansal
34. Thomas J. Watson.
35. iNext
36. 10 great mistakes that Microsoft did.
37. Claude Hopkins

❀ ❀ ❀

Questions

1. The advertising slogans, 'The World's Best Airline', 'We'll Take More Care Of You', 'Fly the Flag', 'The world's favourite airline' belongs to ________.
2. Britisih Airways aeroplanes carried a Union Flag scheme painted on its tail fins. In 1997 the airways made a controversial change from the use of British colours to ethnic Logos. Which rival airways took advantage of this and quickly adopted the British flag along with the slogan 'Britain's national flag carrier'?
3. With which airlines would you associate slogans like, 'Change is in the air', 'You're there', 'Reaching destinations with more comfort' and 'Excellence in air'?
4. Which company's old slogan 'the possibilities are infinite' is often found below the Logo in major advertisements?
5. Who coined the advertising slogan, 'You press the button and we do the rest'?
6. Which company made use of the advertising campaign 'Forever new Frontiers'?
7. For which product was the slogan, "You'll wonder where the yellow went" coined by Foote, Cone and Blender?
8. The phrase 'Don't leave home without it' is an advertisement campaign done in 1975 by David Ogilvy for ________.
9. Which company recently dropped its 82-year-old slogan 'A glass and a half of full cream milk in every half pound'; one of the reasons being that the present product was weighing 49 gm. or 230 gm.?
10. Which car was positioned as a protest against the vulgarity of Detroit cars in those days with the 'Think Small', campaign by Bill Bernbach and became a cult among those Americans who eschewed conspicuous consumption?

11. For which company was the diabolical positioning, 'When you're only number 2, you try harder, Or else', created by Doyle Dane Bernbach?
12. Which eatery chain created the 'Where is the beef?' television commercial written by Cliff Freeman?
13. Which product has the marketing slogan 'the tool kit in a can'?
14. What was the name of the telephone service planned by Motorola to link up earth with 66 low orbit satellites and launched with the tag-line 'Geography is History'?
15. Who is the creator and lead developer of Gmail, and who is also the founder of Friend Feed and the man behind Google's motto 'Don't be evil'?
16. Which coffee is being advertised with slogans such as, 'Good Just Got Great' and 'Good to the Last Drop'?
17. The Thums Up caption of 80s, 'Happy days are here again' was coined by ________.
18. Your vision, our future is the tagline for ________.
19. Who coined the 'Just do it' slogan for Nike?
20. No Confusion – Great Combination
21. Jaago-Re
22. Your Potential, Our Passion
23. The Power of Dreams
24. Innovation delivered
25. Gateway of India to the World
26. Friday Dressing
27. Where India Shops
28. Power is nothing without control
29. The man of Substance
30. A Great Way to Fly
31. Smooth as Silk
32. Emotionally Yours
33. There is no better way to life
34. Redefined Aggression
35. Satyam Sivam Sundaram
36. Inspire the Next
37. Born 1820 – Still going strong
38. Transforming Tomorrow
39. For the self-made

40. For managing tomorrow
41. ...the name you can bank upon
42. Good people to bank with
43. Build a better life around us
44. Dressing up new India
45. A passion to perform
46. Invented for life
47. Obsessed with quality
48. The world's local bank
49. It takes a licking and keeps on ticking
50. Where's the beef?
51. Let your fingers do the walking
52. Think Small/Drivers wanted
53. It's all about Imagineering
54. We fly for your smile
55. Fresh fashion
56. The secret of style
57. Build a better life around us
58. High Performance Delivered
59. Good people to bank with
60. Genuine since 1937
61. We turn on ideas
62. Resources are limited; Creativity is unlimited

Answers

1. British Airways
2. Virgin Atlantic
3. Royal Jordanian Airlines
4. Fujitsu
5. George Eastman, Eastman's Kodak
6. Boeing
7. Pepsodent
8. American Express Travellers' cheque
9. Cadbury Dairy Milk Chocolate (it made no sense to stick to the tag-line as a Cadbury bar was weighing 49 gm. or 230 gm.)
10. Volkswagen

11. Avis
12. Wendy's
13. 3 in 1 oil
14. Iridium
15. Paul Buchheit
16. Maxwell House
17. Vasant Kumar
18. OLYMPUS
19. Dan Wieden
20. ITC Bingo
21. Tata Tea
22. Microsoft
23. Honda
24. Accenture
25. VSNL
26. Allen Solly
27. Pantaloons
28. Pirelli Tyre Company
29. Graviera Suitings
30. Singapore Airlines
31. Thai Airways
32. Air Sahara
33. Lufthansa
34. Ford Mondeo
35. Doordharshan
36. Hitachi
37. Johny Walker whisky
38. Arcelor Mittal
39. Grasim Suitings
40. Business Today
41. Punjab National Bank
42. Union Bank of India
43. Central Bank of India
44. Vimal
45. Deutsche Bank
46. Bosch

47. Skoda
48. HSBC
49. Timex
50. Wendy's
51. Yellow Pages
52. Volkswagen
53. Larsen & Toubro
54. Austrian
55. Pantaloons
56. OCM Suiting
57. Central Bank of India
58. Accenture
59. Union Bank of India
60. Rayban
61. Seagate
62. Posco

Questions

1. Name the famous brand character produced by Frederick William Rueckheim and his brother Louis in 1893 for the "Candied Popcorn and Peanuts". This company was later purchased by Borden and sold to Frito-Lay.
2. This character made his debut in 1969 as a cartoon spokesman by Anheuser-Busch and became the official mascot with the tagline 'Dauntless defender of Quality'. Later he was realized as a character Stein of the company in 1975 and was first produced by the firm of Ceremarte of Brazil. Who is this?
3. This mascot was created by Richard McDonald in 1948 who established the principles of the modern fast-food restaurant. Name this original mascot of McDonald's, a man with a chef's hat on top of a hamburger shaped head.
4. Barry Klein, advertisement executive and Willard Scott, a Bozo performer created a morph of Bozo with a crude costume of a paper cup as a nose and a cardboard tray as a hat. The corporate hired Mr. Polakovs, a circus performer to restylized this character's look that emerged into the familiar white-faced clown in a canary-yellow jumpsuit and a fire-engine red wig. Name the famous brand character ________.
5. An anthropomorphic pink rabbit was created in 1973 and used as a species to promote a brand of batteries. This was originally trademarked for use in the US and other countries. The company lost it as they failed to renew its US trademark and the rival grabbed the opportunity and trademarked it for its use ________.
6. Eric Allard, a special effects expert from All Effects Company created this marketing icon with a pink rabbit wearing sunglasses and blue sandals that beats a bass drum. DDB Chicago advertising produced this ad commercial in 1989 as a parody of its rivals TV commercial. Name the icon ________.

7. An American entrepreneur with his Original Recipe founded this chain of restaurants. He partnered with Pete Harman to launch his first restaurant in 1952. His image is omnipresent in his chain's advertising and packaging. Who is he?
8. He was a muscular, tanned, bald man with a hoop earing and a no non-sense attitude towards dirt and grime. His original was a US Navy Sailor from Florida. The famous TV actor House Peters Jr. played the live role of this mascot during late 1950s and early 1960s. Who is he?
9. Her name was first coined by the Washburn Crosby Company in 1921. She hosted radio programmes in 1924. She is named the second most popular American woman in 1945 by *Fortune Magazine*. Her image became the cultural icon for General Mills. Who is she?
10. He won the battle with Katty the Kangaroo, Elmo the Elephant and Newt the Gnu for advertising this company's product in 1952. He was accompanied by Hanna-Barbera characters Huckleberry Hound and Snagglepuss. He became the cereal icon for the company and gave the product a voice, a face and a name. Name the company and the icon.
11. What is the formal name of the advertising icon and the mascot "Pillsbury Doughboy"?
12. Antonio Gentile, a fourteen-year school boy created this Logo in a contest held by the Planters, an American snack-food company. It also appeared as an animated cartoon character in TV commercials.
13. Nipper dog is used as an advertising icon for which company?
14. What is the name of the mascot of *Chandamama* magazines?
15. Shepton Dash was for the first eight years the brand mascot for this product. His successor was the still more famous Fernville Lord Digby who also made his owner Cynthia Harrison famous. The brand mascots of this products have been breed champions and five of them have won 'Best of Show' prizes. Identify the brand _________.
16. Which company's Logo was called the 'Gold Guy' which consisted of a crude gold coloured figure resembling a petroglyph standing on a purple letter 'L' inscribed with the company's name?
17. For which product was the striding man Logo created by Tom Browne?
18. Which product had the rooster mascot named Fresh-Up Freddie?
19. Name the company with the four leaf clover Logo?
20. With which product do you associate the symbol of sword in a rounded device with the brand name in the centre?
21. Which brand of paint has an old English sheepdog as its brand mascot?

22. With which brand of Kimberly Clerk is the Labrador retriever puppy synonymous with?
23. For which product is 'Chimpoo' the mascot?
24. What is the symbol of WWF's worldwide conservation efforts to save life on earth?
25. Who is the personality known to the world as 'Onida Devil'?
26. The green rooster named Cornelius was the mascot of ________.
27. Who created the triangle faced Fido Dido the mascot of 7 Up?
28. Louis is the name of the mnemonic of ________.
29. "Ahem Bugged" is the original name of which animated character, shown in the advertisement of a popular brand?
30. Videocon introduced a new brand identity for its consumer durables division; an electric green Logo composed of two animated characters named ________.
31. Name the famous cow created for Borden in 1930s with beautiful smile and fresh daisies around her neck which symbolize the fresh dairy quality and she is the spokescow for Borden Dairy Foods since 1938 ________.
32. Which cartoon character shares its name with a mascot used by British Airways?
33. Whose TV commercial featured a character called Mr. Dirt to portray the damaging effects that dirt had on automobile engines?
34. Which company made a series of cartoon advertisements using a character called, 'Chunder Loo of Akim Foo' in the Sydney Bulletin?
35. "He may look like royalty, but he isn't royal" were the famous words of Bobby Kooka who conceived this icon or character. Who is this character?
36. Which company used Dr. Rabbits World tour and Dr. Rabbit and the Legend of the Tour Kingdom to teach about dental health and to advertise their toothpaste ________.

Answers

1. Cracker Jack
2. The Bud Man
3. Speedee
4. Ronald McDonald
5. Duracell Bunny
6. Energizer Bunny

7. Harland Davis Sanders popularly known as Colonel Sanders who founded Kentucky Fried Chicken
8. Mr. Clean, Procter & Gamble
9. Betty Crocker
10. Tony the Tiger, Kellog's Frosted Flakes
11. Poppin Fresh
12. Mr. Peanut
13. RCA Victor
14. Baba the Bunny
15. Dulux and its brand mascot Dulux dog
16. Lucas Arts
17. Johnny Walker
18. 7 Up
19. Religare
20. Dettol
21. Dulux
22. Andrex
23. Garware Paints
24. Giant Panda
25. David Whitbread
26. Kellog's Cornflakes
27. Joanna Ferrone. Fido is India's first animated mascot who sang, danced, joked, laughed and cried with its audience
28. Mortein brand
29. Vicks Khitch-Khitch
30. Chouw and Mouw
31. Elsie
32. Dilbert
33. Mobil
34. Cobra Boot Polish
35. Air India Maharaja
36. Colgate Toothpaste

❀ ❀ ❀

Questions

1. This Logo was created by Art Paul with a black bunny head wearing a tuxedo bow tied that represents the playful character of a famous magazine. This Logo was never altered till today since its creation ________.
2. The shape of this Logo represents the wing in the renowned statue of the Greek Goddess of Victory ________.
3. Name the bowtie Logo of the automobile industry ________.
4. Name the Logo that has a puzzled sphere with few missing pieces ________.
5. This motorcycle company uses the symbol tuning fork in its Logo to represent their presence in the musical instruments ________.
6. Name the 'Gemini' or 'Twins' Logo of Richard Branson's company designed by the English artist and illustrator, Roger Dean that has been replaced in 1979 ________.
7. This green and silver coloured 3D sphere Logo represents the joint venture of two great companies with the alphabets ________.
8. Which Logo is a combination of four religious symbols: Star of David, the Christian Cross, the Wicca and the Islamic Crescent Moon?
9. Which company's Logo features a flying Seagull?
10. Which automobile company has the red coloured rhombus shape?
11. Name the company's Logo that features a siren, twin-tailed mermaid ________.
12. This chocolate company hails from The City of Bears and the Logo is designed by featuring a silhouette of a bear ________.
13. Which company has the wing foot Logo?
14. Which company's Logo is called "emsignia"?
15. Which bird was featured in Mclaren's original Logo designed by Michael Turner?

16. What is the meaning of 'AKAI' which is also indicated through its Logo?
17. What is common between the four Logos that have been designed for United Parcel Service?
18. Which famous studio has a lady carrying a torch and draped in The American flag as its Logo?
19. Whose Logo consists of an apple, green grapes, leaves, purple grapes and gooseberry?
20. Which company was founded in 1916 as an aircraft engine manufacturer whose Logo symbolizes an aircraft propeller while the colours allude to the blue and white checkered flag of Bavaria?
21. Which pharma major has as its Logo, the Apis Bull, which is workshipped as the incarnation of Ptah the creator of the universe?
22. Which airline is identified by the blue globe Logo and the use of the word clipper in its aircraft's names?
23. Which airlines during its formation had the sea horse Logo, known as the hippocampe aile?
24. Which spirits company uses the bat Logo along with the phrase, "company founded in Santiago De Cuba in 1862"?
25. Which airlines has the hammer and sickle Logo?
26. The Edelweiss flower was the Logo of Swarovski and at present it has been changed to a bird. Which bird is the Logo of Swarovski?
27. Whose Logo was designed by Ruth Kedar and is a word mark based on catull typeface?
28. Who uses the custom typeface Norad for branding their Logo?
29. For which product did Henry Alexander a British artist design the walking fingers Logo and whose tagline created eight years later was, 'Let your fingers do the walking'?
30. Which company's new version of Logo was designed by Paul Rand in 1972 in which horizontal stripes replaced solid letters to suggest speed and dynamism?
31. What is the colour of the 'l' in Google Logo?
32. Which company has the double horsemen Logo, an iconic mark of one horseman playing another?
33. Whose Logo was an inspiration from a painting by English artist Francis Barraud which was that of a dog listening to a cylindrical phonogram?
34. Which group has launched a refurbished Logo, peacock in vibrant red, reflecting the strength and energy radiated by the group and a

unique lower case style in which the company's name is given and brand campaign built around the theme 'energy unbound'?

35. Who painted the Dutch boy used as a trademark and Logo by Dutch boy that made paints, modelled after an Irish-American boy who lived near the place of domicile of the artist?
36. What does the four rings in the AUDI Logo symbolize?
37. What is the name of Google Logo that involves modifications of their Logo for use on holidays, birthdays of famous people and major events?
38. Which company was started in 1913 by Archibald Tuft, Hughes, Charles, Myers and Hussey and featured a diamond shaped Logo, and the diamond shape persists in its branding till today?
39. Which truck company's Logo is a chrome plated bull dog, which can be found in the front of all its trucks?
40. This automaker's badge was designed in 1910 by draughtsman Romano Cattaneo who shows two heraldic devices with Biscione, the emblem of the House of Visconti, rulers of Milan in the 14th Century on the right and a red cross on a white field, the emblem of Milan on the left. In 1918 a dark blue metallic ring was added along with its name and Milano. Minor changes to the badge was again made in 1925 and 1946. Identify the automaker _________.
41. The third United Parcel Service Logo which had the iconic package and shield was designed by _________.
42. Who was the business strategy consultant who gave Wipro its visual identity comprising the rainbow flower and the 'Applying Thought' base line?
43. Who designed the Logo of JCB?
44. Which organization's visual identity demonstrating the organization's DNA – Imagination, Action and Joy was designed by Chetan a student of the Spastic Society of Karnataka?
45. The 'Leo the Lion' MGM Logo originally introduced in 1924 was designed by a publicist for the studio named _________.
46. Which pen company made use of the white dot trademark?
47. Which hotel chain's Logo featured a friendly bald innkeeper, dubbed 'Uncle Ben' who sported an apron and who held a top hat in one hand and a red trumpeted banner that read the hotel's name in the other hand?
48. Whose Logo is a stylized representation of the Greek God of fire and forge, Hephaestos (Roman Vulcan) the muscular male arm with hammer in fist and which was also the symbol of the Socialist Labour Party of America?

49. Which utensil is depicted on the Logo of the ecomark scheme in India?
50. The company's Logo is a white star resembling the top of a snow capped mountain peak. Which company am I talking about?
51. Which Indian conglomerate's Logo represents fluid motion and was designed by Wolf Olins?
52. Which stationery brand chose something as a symbol "due to its capacity to endure long periods of difficulty"?
53. Why did the Godrej Logo, just had a change of colour when they wanted to make it contemporary without involving any design change?
54. Which automobile has the Griffin emblem taken from the coat of arms of a mercenary soldier who was granted the manor of Luton for services to King John in the Thirteenth Century?
55. Which entity has the card Logo resembling a Venn diagram with the tagline 'the heart of commerce'?
56. Who was the first computer maker to use the Intel Logo on its products from the time of its launch?
57. What is the icon developed for cruelty free product?
58. Which is the first premium brand of diamond jewellery in the world to employ Ion Beam branding technology for branding their Logo?
59. Who designed the Pac-Man Logo of Microsoft?
60. Name the web browser that used the Firebird/Phoenix as its Logo during its evolution ________.
61. Which auto company has the winged arrow as its central part of the Logo?

Answers

1. Playboy America's best selling magazine
2. Nike popularly known as 'Swoosh'
3. Chevrolet
4. Wikipedia
5. Yamaha
6. Virgin
7. Sony Ericson
8. Disturbed, American heavy metal rock band
9. Hollister Company, an American lifestyle brand
10. Mitsubishi Motors
11. Starbucks Corporation, a coffeehouse chain

12. Toblerone
13. GoodYear
14. Motorola
15. Kiwi Bird
16. Red
17. They all share the shield theme
18. Columbia Pictures
19. Fruit of the Loom
20. BMW
21. Nova Nordisk
22. PanAm
23. Air France
24. Bacardi
25. Areoflot
26. Swan
27. Google
28. Android
29. Yellow Pages
30. IBM
31. Green
32. US Polo
33. His Master's Voice
34. Murugappa Group
35. Lawrence Carmichael Earle
36. Indicates the union of four founder companies – Audi, Horsh, DKW and Wanderer Automobile
37. Google Doodle
38. Clorox
39. Mack Trucks
40. Alfa Romeo
41. Paul Rand
42. Shombit Sengupta founder of Shining Consulting
43. Leslie Smith
44. MindTree
45. Howard Dietz
46. Sheaffer

47. Ramada
48. Arm and Hammer
49. Earthern pot
50. Mont Blanc
51. TATA
52. Camlin – It chose camel as a symbol for its capacity to endure long periods of difficulty
53. The Logo is the founder Ardeshir Godrej's Logo
54. Vauxhall
55. Master Card
56. IBM
57. Small Rabbit
58. Scintilla Monaco
59. Scott Baker
60. Mozilla Firefox
61. Skoda

Questions

Identify the Companies8/Brands' Represented by These Logos

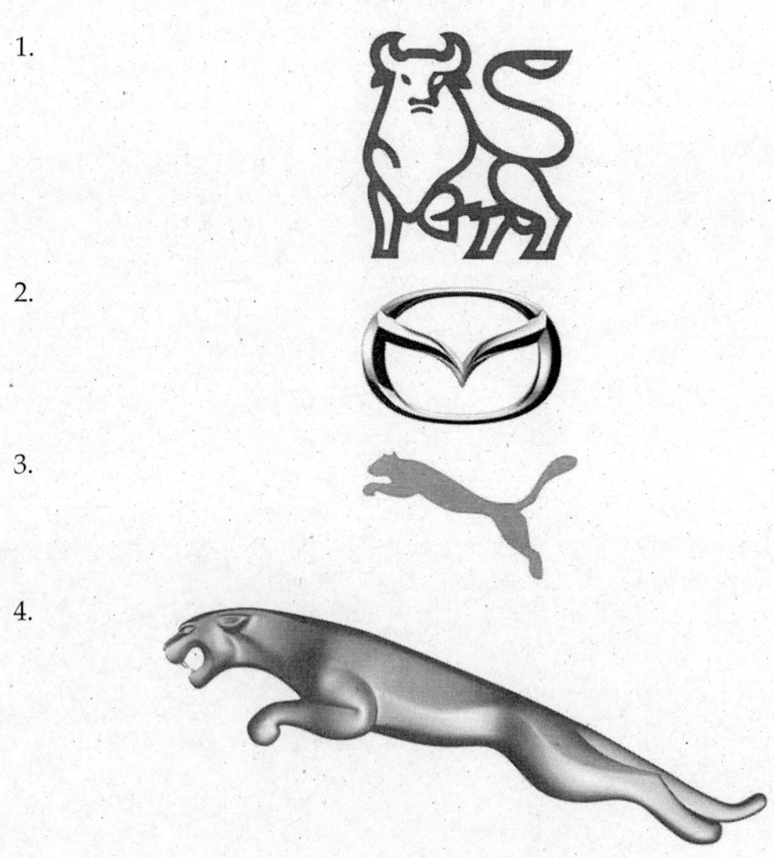

5.

6.

7.

8.

9.

10.

11.

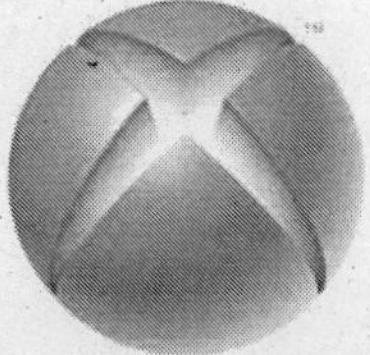

12.

13.

14.

15.

16.

17.

18.

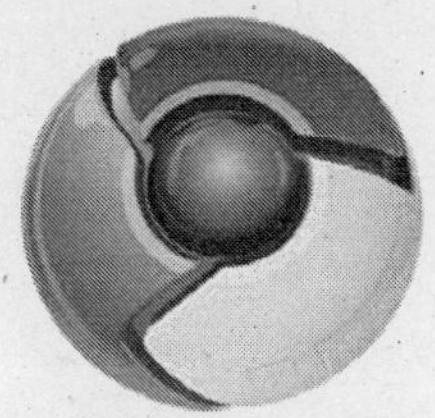

19.

20.

21.

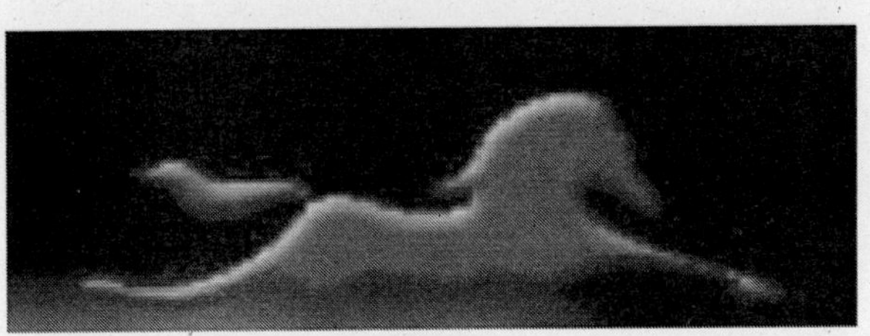

22.

23.

24.

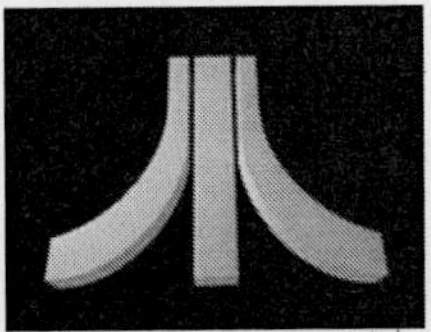

25.

26.

27.

28.

29.

30.

31.

32.

33.

34.

35.

36.

37.

38.

39.

40.

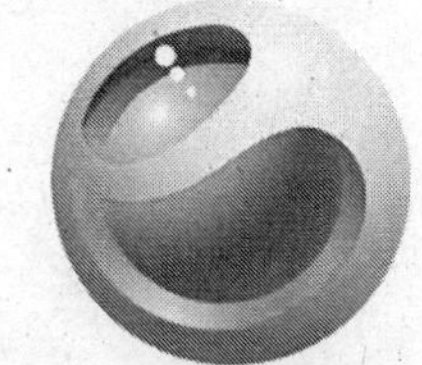

41.

42.

43.

44.

45.

46.

47.

48.

49.

50.

51.

52.

53.

54.

55.

56.

57.

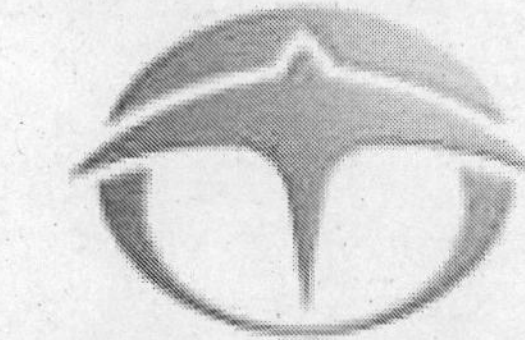

58.

59.

60.

61.

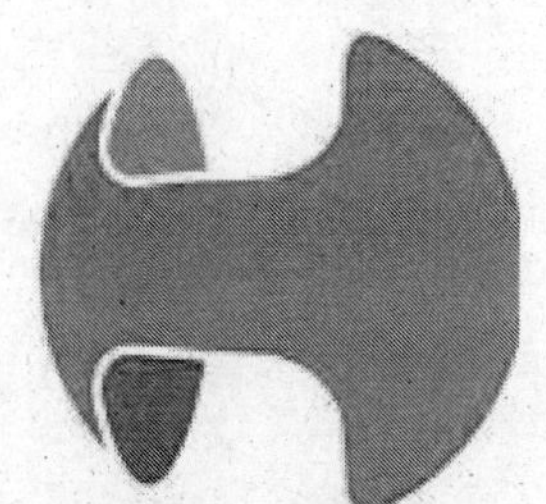

62.

63.

64.

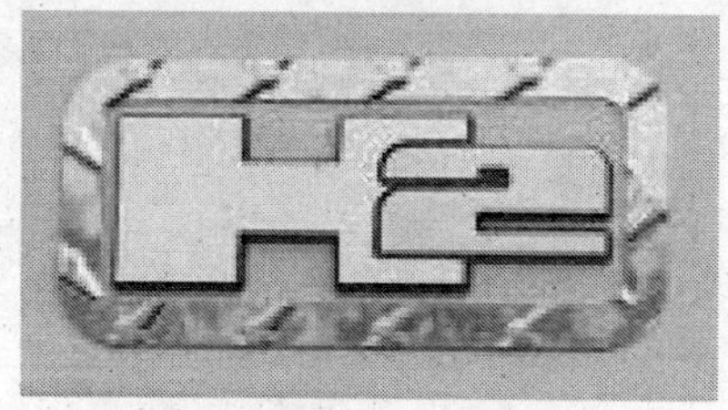

65.

66.

67.

68.

69.

70.

71.

72.

73.

74.

75.

76.

77.

78.

79.

80.

81.

82.

83.

84.

85.

86.

87.

88.

89.

90.

91.

92.

93.

94.

95.

96.

97.

98.

99.

100.

101.

102.

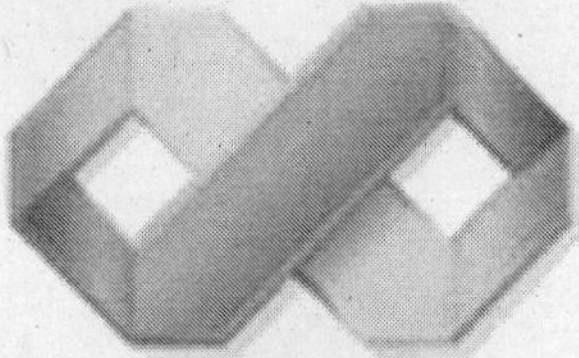

103.

104.

105.

106.

107.

108.

109.

110.

111.

112.

113.

114.

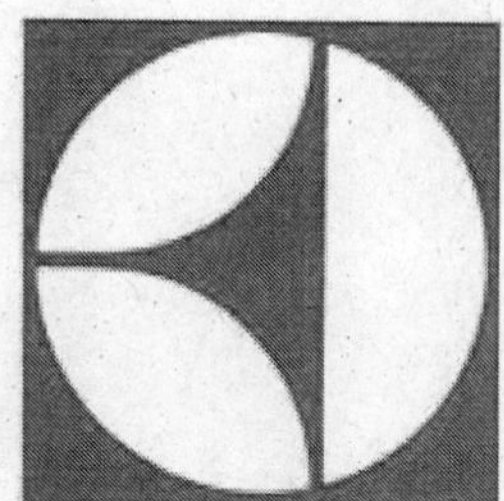

115.

116.

117.

118.

119.

120.

121.

Connect the Logos to find the present name of the company

122. 

1970-1980s Logo

1990s-2000 Logo

123. 

124. 

125.

126. Which product was advertised along with a portrait of Her Majesty Marie, the Queen of Romania done by Philip A De Laszlo as what she kept for her constant use on her dressing table?

127. Taking the cue that photo on the left is that of Chester Carlson whose commercial invention comes from the Greek for 'dry writing'. Identify the significance of the text on the right.

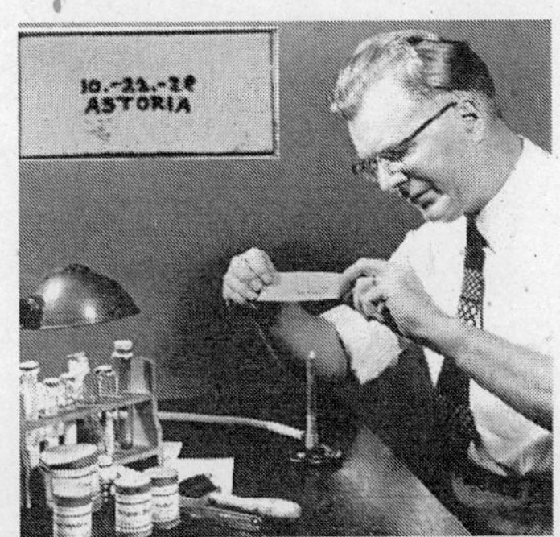

Fun with Doodles

Identify the significance/occasions represented by these doodles

1.

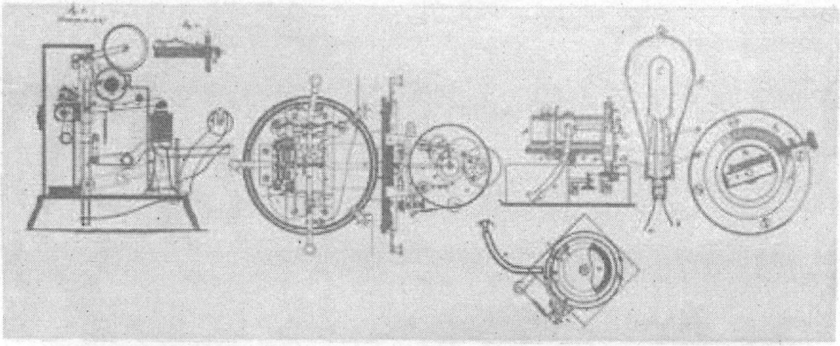

2.

3.

4.

5.

6.

7.

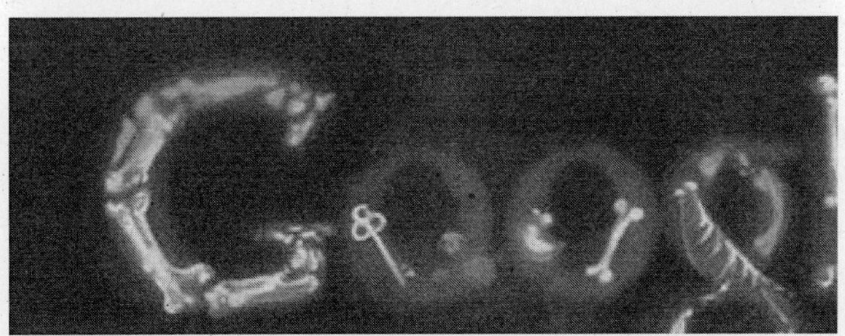

8.

9.

10.

11.

12.

13.

14.

15.

16.

Answers

Logo Questions

1. Merrill Lynch
2. Mazda
3. Puma
4. Jaguar
5. Firefox Logo
6. Tilaknagar Industries
7. Porsche
8. Oldsmobile
9. Cadillac
10. Haggen Daz
11. Xbox
12. Cavinkare
13. Airtel
14. Samsonite
15. Bacardi
16. Boeing
17. Dream Works Animation
18. Google Chrome
19. John Deere
20. Mahindra

21. TVS Motor Company
22. Lowenbrau
23. Videocon
24. Atari
25. Radico Khaitan
26. Bank of Baroda
27. Canara Bank
28. Eveready
29. Lufthansa
30. Benetton
31. Adidas
32. Airbus
33. American Express
34. Citroen
35. AMD
36. Procter and Gamble
37. Double Bull
38. Renault
39. Subaru
40. Sony Erickson
41. Symantec
42. Tommy Hilfiger
43. Thai Airways
44. Swarovski
45. Starbucks
46. Playboy
47. Rover
48. Walmart
49. Motorola
50. Yamaha
51. Xerox
52. Linux
53. Lacoste
54. CNBC
55. Piaggio
56. Sula Wine

57. Avia
58. Daihatsu
59. Dodge
60. Fabrica D, Armi Pietro Beretta
61. Havells
62. Holden
63. HSBC
64. Hummer
65. ING
66. Kelvinator
67. Koenigsegg
68. Lada
69. DBS
70. Accor
71. Escorts
72. Saturn
73. The Sunday Times
74. Syndicate Bank
75. Times of India
76. Yugo
77. Ambuja Cement
78. BNP Paribas
79. Chettinad Cements
80. Coromandel Cement
81. Etisalat
82. Indian Express Group
83. Jockey
84. Jhonson Tiles
85. Legrand
86. Malayalam Manorama
87. Ramraj Cotton
88. The Hindu
89. UCO Bank
90. Zuari Cement
91. IndusInd Bank
92. Alfa Romeo

93. Buick
94. Cadillac
95. Benz
96. Peugeot
97. Adobe Systems
98. Air Deccan
99. Central Bank of India
100. Readers Digest
101. Brittanica
102. Microsoft Visual Studio
103. Reid & Taylor
104. Gatorede
105. Seagate
105. Carrefour
107. Cocochannel
108. Toblerone
109. Volcom
110. Aston Martin
111. Carlsberg
112. Chase Manhattan Bank
113. Danone Corporation
114. Electrolux
115. Chevron
116. UniLever
117. Man
118. Scannia Trucks
119. Porshe
120. Bosch
121. Hapang- Lloyd
122. Vauxhall
123. IBM
124. Union Bank of India
125. Skoda
126. Pond's Cream
127. The first message to be photocopied

Answers for Fun with Doodles

1. Thomas Edison's 164th birthday
2. Cezanne's 172nd Birthday
3. Festival of Kites (India) Jan. 14, 2011
4. New Years Day, January 01, 2011
5. D4G India Winner/Children's Day – (India) November 14, 2010
6. Robert Louis Stevenson's 160th birthday, November 13, 2010
7. Discovery of X-rays, November 8, 2010
8. World Cup Final, July 11, 2010
9. Mother's Day, May 09, 2010
10. Happy Father's Day, June 20, 2010
11. Earth Day, April 22, 2010
12. Holy Festival India, March 01, 2010
13. Happy Valentines Day, February 14, 2007
14. Happy April Fools, April 01, 2007
15. 2008 Beijing Olympics Closing Ceremony, April 24, 2008
16. Google's 10th birthday

❀ ❀ ❀